I0428021

Altered States:

Making the Extraordinary

Ordinary Again

John G. Sabol

Ghost Excavation Research Center

Also by John Sabol

Ghost Excavator (2007)

Ghost Culture (2007)

Gettysburg Unearthed (2007)

Battlefield Hauntscape (2008)

The Anthracite Coal Region (2008)

The Politics of Presence (2008)

Bodies of Substance, Fragments of Memory (2009)

Phantom Gettysburg (2009)

Digging Deep (2009)

The Re-Haunting(s) of Gettysburg (2010)

The Haunted Theatre (2011)

Ghost Culture Too (2012)

Beyond the Paranormal (2012)

Digging-Up Ghosts (2nd publishing, 2013)

Burnside Bridge (2013)

The Gettysburg Experience (2013)

The Absence Above, A Presence Below (2013)

The Production of Haunted Space (2013)

Centralia, Pennsylvania (2013)

The Ghost Excavation (2013)

The Good Death and the Civil War (2014)

Centralia: A Vision of Ruin (2014)

Altered States:

Making the Extraordinary Ordinary Again

Ghost Excavator Books, Inc.TM©

Bedford, Pennsylvania, USA

Altered States: Making the Extraordinary Ordinary Again
~ John G. Sabol ~

Copyright 2014 by John G. Sabol and Ghost Excavation Books, Inc., Bedford, PA, USA. All rights reserved.

Front cover design by Mary Becker, USA. Front cover photos: "Haunted House" stock footage and personal photos of Mary Becker/John Sabol "Glastonbury Abbey" Somerset, England. Back cover design and photo credit: Mary Becker, USA.

The right of John G. Sabol to be identified as the author of the text concepts has been asserted in accordance with section 77 and 78 of the Copyright, Design & Patent Act 1988.

Warning, the text herein is fully protected by U.S. Federal copyright laws. Federal copyright laws will be vigorously enforced and infringement will be prosecuted to the fullest extent of the law, which can include damages and lawyer's fees to be paid by the infringer of copyright. No part of this book may be reproduced or transmitted in any form or by any means, electronic or mechanical, including photocopying, recording or by any information storage and retrieval system without written permission from the publisher. For additional copyright information contact Ghost Excavation Books, Inc., at ghost.excavation@yahoo.com.

All names and original photos are used with permission and copyrighted by their respective owners. "The Haunted House © 2004 Daniele Montella" image is provided by "Fanpop". Historical photos provided by Photo Archive.

ISBN-13: 978-1500166311
ISBN-10: 1500166316

Ghost Excavation Books, Inc. ™©
A division of C.A.S.P.E.R. Research Center™©,
Bedford, PA, USA
www.ghostexcavation.com

"The present is full of ruins of the recent past and they epitomize the fragility of boundaries....and the materials for a haunting awareness of what forces may still linger in signs and traces".

- Barry Curtis, *Dark Places: The Haunted House in Film* (2008: 222).

Acknowledgements

This book would not be possible without thanking individuals who participated during a "Ghost Excavation". This involved a concerted <u>team</u> effort. It was characterized by a firm commitment by all involved to gather contextual data through the various performances of resonating cultural acts. Each investigator, in their own unique way, accurately recorded the multitude of sensory elements that continuously manifested as a result of making what is thought to be extraordinary, ordinary.

I wish to personally thank each team member for their enormous efforts during these "excavations"! A big thanks and a warm embrace to (and in no particular order):

James McCann   Mike "Herman" Stevenson
Joseph Andrasi   Jason Jarvie
James Castle   Brian Parsons
Matt James   Brandy Williams
Jonathan Williams   Alex Matsuo
Renee Cannon
                 AND...
                 Mary Becker

A Haunting Invitation

Let us who do this fieldwork labor not rest merely in the shade of traditional performances and practices. Let us slowly, meticulously, abandon the strings of an attachment to the culture we have built out of current scientific views of reality and a TV "boob-tube". Let us live that "other" reality, often hidden and frequently distained as a "fringe" pursuit, and one seldom fully explored. Let us begin, if it must be solo, alone, independent, taking heart of what we experience, and not be concerned what contemporary others might think of us:

"I here live and do not scramble to fit myself to the requirements of others. In a narrow tomb….I have just room for my bed. Behind me is that Great Peace the Desert".

- **Flinders Petrie, archaeologist**

Let us enter that "Desert" together now. Though it is a place devoid of life on the surface, it teems with the remains of past presence beneath the surface of things.

Let's begin to re-populate it with new ideas, concepts, and methods. And let's begin now!

Preface

"The study of science is different....it begins with legends and oversimplifications...details are added, complexities are engaged, unanswerable questions begin to be posed. A scientific account is a story which can always be retold, for the line of the narrative in scientific writing is to be found in the deepening of the concept".

- **Norman Mailer,** *Of a Fire on the Moon*

Sometimes, one "digs deep" to simplify things. And the route to a scientific breakthrough is not always measured on the surface of things. In ghost research, this breakthrough, I propose, is not through the "paranormal", something beyond normal. It does not connect with supernatural agents, "somebodies" who are above (or below) the natural. A clear path can be traversed within the depth that is the surface of the everyday, where the normal and the natural occur, and have always occurred.

A belief in "ghosts", "spirits", and something that "haunts" is <u>not</u> associated with un(under)-developed technologies, sciences, or educational systems, and largely believed as a cultural system in Third World countries traditionally studied by cultural anthropologists. Humans use both analytical and intuitive systems of meaning, sometimes occurring simultaneously, and further

"the finding that paranormal beliefs mainly arise from an intuitive system, instead of a malfunctioning analytical system, explains why the beliefs do not vanish with the increase of education, scientific knowledge, and rational thinking" (Aarnio 2007:6).

There is no secret formula or electronic device that unlocks the past, just something that has been lost and forgotten in time, space, and this technological age. It hints of a simple, yet more enriched view of life, where connections and interactions between human, animal, and the "other" are frequent and sociable. This is a science that touches multiple entities, all of which is normal and natural. There is no "para-mentality" or super-scientism at work in the field. It is extra workings and a hosting that expands and deepens the consciousness of what it is to feel and be human, as well as interact with the humanity that has always surrounded us.

Anthropologist Clifford Geertz has effectively argued that **"there is no such thing as a human nature independent of culture".** If "ghosts" were once human, and not supernatural or demonic entities, then the investigation of their hauntings should be cultural in nature. But it must be the culture in which the haunting is said to have originated, and not the ambiance of our contemporary, technologically more advanced culture.

The field of inquiry into a cultural haunting, I propose, becomes a series of excavation stories, surface probes that dig deep into the ordinary, the normal, and the natural. As an archaeologist, I participate in history as both an actor and a narrator of what I unearth or re-cover. The archaeological story (as history) is about "what happened" and "that which is said to have happened". In an excavation, there is also another storyline: "that which remains". In the excavation process, the dead can return to haunt "what happened", and our knowledge written in narratives about the history of past events.

A "ghost excavation" is a forensic tool with the intention of uncovering and revealing what lies hidden, lost, or forgotten. Though this lies outside (or underneath) the vision of the contemporary every day, it is still <u>not</u> "paranormal". If it were, then archaeological work would be a "paranormal" exploration!

To assume that something, someone (like a "burial") that lies hidden does not mean that it's "excavation" (or "unearthing") represents a "paranormal" event. It does mean that what is unearthed (what "manifests") may be different from what one encounters in the present. This difference, however, is socio-cultural, not supernatural or demonic.

We must go beyond the concept of a "staged authenticity", saying that this or that is "ghostly" or "paranormal" in origin; or if it is, it is "debunked". We must focus on **"material authenticity" (Karlstrom 2012),** in which **"objects that are true and in their original state".** This immediately eliminates "orbs" and other similar visual phenomena.

This focus on <u>unchanged</u> conditions through time, a "haunting" (even one perceived as "interactive"), eliminates contemporary uses of modern devices. And "playing" with these devices, in the expectation that a past presence will understand (in time) the device's meaning, and willingly respond to "beeps", "colored lights", "sticks" that move, and commands from unknown humans.

A "ghost excavation" explores potential "authenticity" a different way. During a "ghost excavation" (see Sabol 2012; 2013), our sense of place, as some place distinctively past, is never displaced. In the field, we remain in character as that actor immersed in the past, not the present. When manifestations occur, and "remains" are recovered, by remaining in character, a displacement (between present and past) is not felt. This continues our <u>intended</u> identity with the past as a continuous and entangled flow of communicative gestures and actions, <u>without</u> perceiving one to be from the present and the "other" from the past.

This character emplacement in (with) the past, without concerning ourselves with the use of contemporary environmental scans (which displace our identity), reinforces our sense of a connection we make to "what happened here". Performance counts. Measurement, to a past presence, does not! Sociolinguist Dell Hymes, in *In Vein I Tried to Tell You: Essays in Native American Ethnopoetics* (1981), outlines the importance of performance in fieldwork.

He considers the use of performance to be important to the acquisition of cultural competence. And cultural competence is important, I propose, for analyzing a "ghostly" presence in its historical context. According to Hymes, field performance functions to:

- Interpret behavior;
- Report on behavior; and
- Repeat behavior.

These three functions of performance are important in ghost research. And an investigator who is performing, (rather than monitoring a video screen or reading a meter) one **"assumes responsibilities to an audience" (Hymes 1981:84).** That "audience", our "client", is the "ghost", not a contemporary TV audience or You-Tube subscriber. And that audience warrants empathy and a morale code tied to <u>their</u> social structure and system of beliefs!

Performance is part of archaeological fieldwork which, itself, is the study of (and working with) what remains of the past. According to archaeologist Michael Shanks (2012), the archaeologist must **"do something, create an event, a happening, and watch what ensues…." (2012:39).** It is the craft of archaeology, working with what may remain, that is doing something which prompts a connection to be made with what (and sometimes "who") had, until then, been forgotten, lost, or buried. That "happening" becomes a "haunting". And this performed creativity, mentioned by Shanks, is exactly what we do in a "ghost excavation".

The "excavation" becomes a "knowing search" (not a "hunt") with a direction back into the past. It is motivated by what was already there, as researched in the historical narrative. Though fragmented and "buried", it is now, through performance, becoming present as it is "unearthed" in a "ghost excavation".

When one explores and "excavates" a site in "ruin", one perceives and experiences a past culture in decay, fragmented and manifesting as residual trace remains, perhaps some interactive. It is a world in transition. What one confronts in these ruins is how this past culture has (is) fragmented. But, "cultural heritage", in the form of a "haunting", is becoming present, percolating in contemporary reality.

We must "excavate" and preserve this past, not alter (or even destroy) it with inappropriate words, phrases, gestures, demands, or "triggers". A haunting is cultural heritage! Anna Karlstrom, an archaeologist at Uppsala

University, invites us to **"take spirits seriously as constitutive elements of heritage".**

If "ghosts" and "spirits" are a part of cultural heritage, albeit a world heritage, then their continuance and manifestations are not something "paranormal". Should we behave a certain way (with upmost respect and empathy) when encountering them? I propose that we should!

If a "haunting" is cultural heritage, it is not something whimsical, terrifying, or a source of entertainment. What remains in the ruin is a form of human social expression by which cultural transmission is being passed on through time.

The German sociologist Max Weber makes a distinction between two methods in social science. These are explanation and understanding (1947:79-80). According to Weber, an explanation depends upon detecting statistical regularities in behavior that is accounted for in terms of general laws. Understanding, on the other hand, is based on a meaningful interaction with others in order to discover (or recover) the culturally-specific (and contextual) ways in which they exist and make sense of the world. The exploration of a haunting, as part of social science, should focus, I propose, on the understanding of a haunting (as a past trace or fragment of behavioral presence), rather than an explanation of "how" it is occurring (a "paranormal" event).

In a "ghost excavation", we perform contextual cultural scenarios, developed from historical narratives, to aid us in this understanding. If there is a direct (and immediate) contextually-communicative manifestation to our enacted performance, verified by the RT-EVP audio recorder, we have an **"abduction"**. An "abduction" is the logical procedure an investigator can use when they *think* they have detected a meaningful pattern (such as cultural scenario performance= immediate manifesting response) in events, and then acts upon them (communicates to them) (Eco 1990: 59).

The problem in ghost research is that we cannot live in the past. We must ask what understandings are gained from this relationship (this entanglement) between the performance of a contextual cultural scenario and the immediate manifestation of a contextual response. The "abduction" provides a means toward that understanding.

One major difference between archaeological and ghost excavation is that in the former people are always assumed missing. In a "ghost excavation", traces of active presence remain. In a "ghost excavation", sensory manifestations become understood, in some cases, as human cultural agents. Some of the sensory manifestations that we record at haunted sites are inferred ("abducted") social practices and past cultural performances involved ("remembered") in specific situations and acts by particular (past) actors.

A "ghost excavation" allow us to <u>begin</u> to eliminate numerous "fractures" of traditional archaeological excavation:

- The "fracture" of an absent subject;
- The "fracture" of non-observable change; and
- The "fracture" of "anachronism".

A "ghost excavation" seriously engages the absence of presence and intentional agency. We address specific past situations, "targeting" particular biographies of historical (not necessarily "historic") figures. During a "ghost excavation", we observe and/or record something happening (manifesting) in real time: an actual moment of controlled change from a past becoming present. And an absent past presence can be made present by specifically "targeting" ("excavating") a particular strata of past memory of a specific individual or individuals (as part of their know biography), deemed from historical research.

Memory is an experience that is preserved in a space-time dimension, a strata (or field) of production. A "ghost" does not continue to learn as much as <u>remember</u>. A haunting, therefore, is a field of remembrance, not learning.

Experience becomes memory. We immerse ourselves, in a "ghost excavation", in past situations of particular events to experience some of those same emotions. This is in the hope of "unearthing" a memory field that remains from the past. Our creative endeavors produce emergent qualities (Sawyer 2003), that is a manifesting presence.

Let's take back the field by exploring the possibilities of past presence through trace and vestige remains. We must understand where the "ghost hunting" and "paranormal culture", its belief systems and its semiotic expressions ("ghost tech") has led us. Let's end the mixing of cultural myth, "legend tripping", New Age philosophies, and mysticism as a form of "object animation" tied to electronic devices.

By promoting our form of fieldwork (as a "ghost excavation"), we promote the human past, not a demonic or supernatural one. By focusing on past ethnographic expressions, we promote human (not "alien" or "paranormal") culture. This intent and research stance requires an altered state of mind and behavior, one that crosses borders. It "jumps the fence" that has restricted our vision of contemporary reality.

The use of acting and actors, a **"theatre/archaeology" (Pearson and Shanks 2001),** to explore a haunting is a conscious choice. This is because an altered state is considered normal in acting (cf. Bates 1986). Besides, an actor exhumes performance energy that attracts entities to them. So, they have to perform to expectations: those of the audience (the "ghosts"). This establishes a <u>past</u> identity, an important concept in a "ghost excavation".

An altered state of consciousness occurs in ghost research when one departs from the popular trope of "ghost hunting" ("scan and demand"). And from what is <u>recognized</u> as "paranormal" beliefs, expectations, expressions, and behaviors of a "ghost hunt culture".

Figure 1: The Flow of an "Altered State"

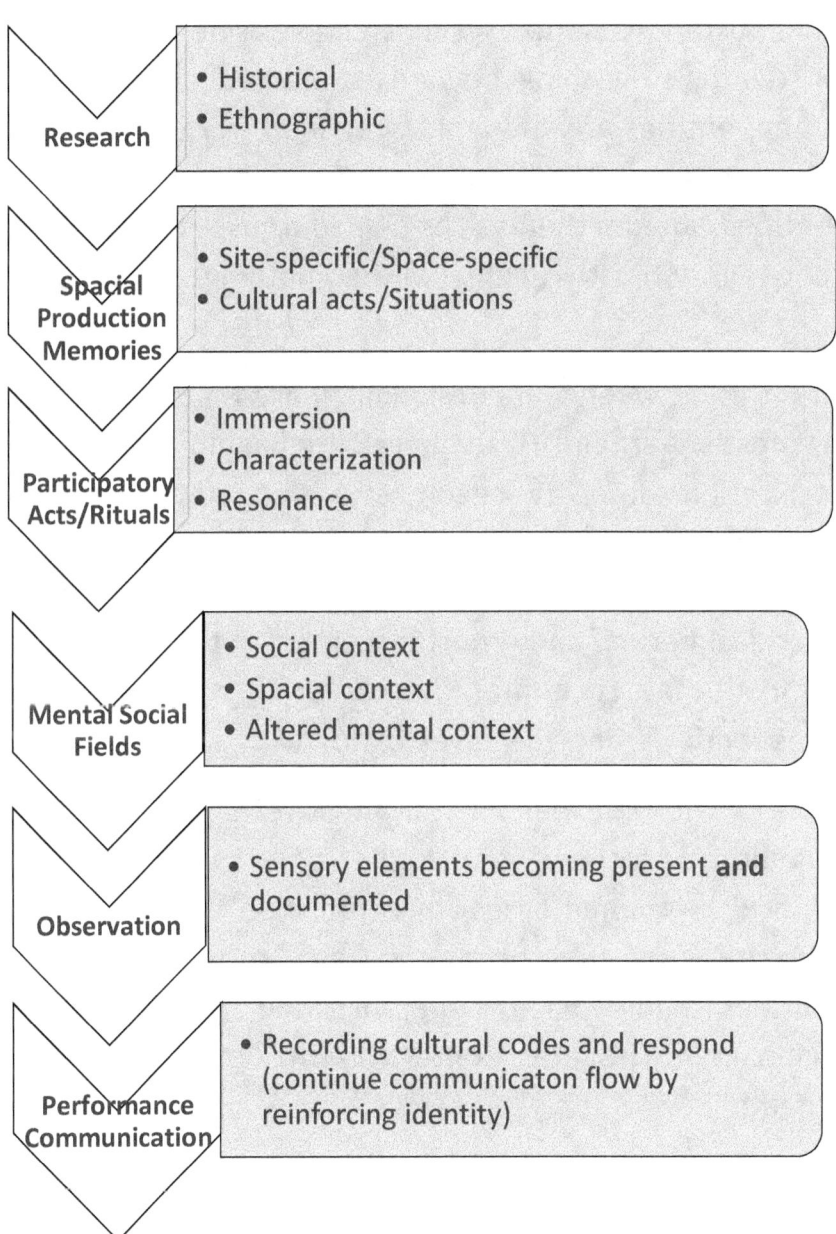

Research
- Historical
- Ethnographic

Spacial Production Memories
- Site-specific/Space-specific
- Cultural acts/Situations

Participatory Acts/Rituals
- Immersion
- Characterization
- Resonance

Mental Social Fields
- Social context
- Spacial context
- Altered mental context

Observation
- Sensory elements becoming present **and** documented

Performance Communication
- Recording cultural codes and respond (continue communicaton flow by reinforcing identity)

Finally, let's take the possibilities of ghostly manifestations seriously! In a catastrophe that results in death, something beyond a peaceful transition in sleep, entities are suddenly wrenched from life as they knew it. In what follows (in some cases and for some), entities can find themselves on a journey, in a transition between what they knew and something as yet to be reached.

It is this between state or liminal phase that the "ghost" is most venerable. This venerability has no set time, or expiration date. It becomes a "haunting". In this transitional phase, the ghost encounters nothing as it was, and what is to come is darkened in mystery. This is a critical period, and unfortunately it is a time when the "ghost" may encounter the casual "ghost hunter" or weekend "paranormal investigator".

One of the principal aims of ghost research, I suggest, should be to show how simple (and how emotionally difficult), in some cases, this transition can be. In this transition, certain behaviors can be vital to these entities trying to find coherence and meaning in the liminality of death (some without knowing this is "death").

Many times today, in particular places popularly labeled "haunted" today; this ghostly transition period is marred by contemporary tropes of ego, economics, and entertainment. The "ghost hunt" hinders this transition with the use of confusing objects (tech devices), and behaviors (making demands and giving commands). Let's stop this "rite of passage" as a "hunt", and begin to act appropriately according to the standards (and memory) of the "ghosts" we seek. After all, who knows when one of us may have a similar "rite of passage" after "passing on"!

Table of Contents

Figures

Photos

Leaping the Fence

"One does what one's time dictates, does one not? One does what one is ordered or expected to do….the unexpected event….leaves one unprepared and fumbling".

- **Loren Eiseley**

Sometimes, we define and adhere to artificial restrictions that limit our vision of space and thought. We impose boundaries that are superficial. Loren Eiseley has said this about boundary-defining parameters:

"one exists in a universe convincingly real, where the lines are sharply drawn in black and white. It is only later, if at all, that one realizes the lines were never there in the first place" (1975:100).

I am particularly concerned about boundary-maintaining regarding our perception (or lack of) haunted landscapes. This concerns both the world of "paranormal culture" and the world of academia. Donald Meinig (1979) has said that **"landscape is defined by our vision and interpreted by our minds. It**

is a panorama which continuously changes as we move along any route (1979:3).

Far too often our vision has been restricted, our mind "fenced-in", as we have taken a particular route to (and in) a landscape perceived as "haunted", a landscape said to be occupied by "ghosts". This "haunted landscape" can be viewed as a popular contemporary cultural template in which a sense of place, and experiences in that space, become bounded, restricting movement and perception, with an overt sensitivity (albeit pre-established) as to "what" and "who" are there.

Yentsch (1988) investigated the way material culture, in the form of old houses, have been used to create an ideology that uses physical remains as the mechanism for meaning. She demonstrated that material culture can be an active agent through which mytho-history is told to succeeding generations. As historic sites deteriorate, more and more their function as historical or cultural markers become lost, and the "ghost hunt" takes precedence, based on what is visibly present, and what is perceived as absent presence.

This semiotic struggle between myth and history, the "paranormal" and cultural remains, is a struggle for control of the way the events of the past (as a "haunting") are interpreted (see Linenthal 1991). The "paranormal turn" at many of these once neglected and forgotten sites does not, in many instances, have anything to do with historical "ghosts". They are "marked" as such for a particular contemporary reason: economic interests as "ghost tourism" or a catalyst for popular "edutainment".

A particular segment of a society's fear, and attraction to that fear, can be observed through this material culture of old, abandoned buildings, and its architectural decay, more so than its history. When these remains become part of a site's mythology, they become subject to a myth-making process.

Photo 1: The Haunted House Motif

Any attempt to cover or contain the flow of experience about life, death, and what remains with finite and bounded terms and concepts is an absurd view of reality. Lives (past/present/future) are not limited (or limiting), and the world that remains from the past, like its contemporary counterpart, is never something finished. There is always a making (or re-making), a future vision, and changing courses of action.

When one establishes boundaries, defining notions of presence and absence as concrete examples "set in stone", putting up fences of resistance, restricting one's vision, all of these become limiting measures, decreasing our understanding of what remains from the past. We must avoid reductions and generalizations which claim to capture the essence of what we are observing and recording. This doesn't answer questions. It builds walls around understanding.

We need a border-crossing. We must shift our fieldwork from cause (or goal) to consequence: what effect do our acts and behaviors in the field have on what we are attempting to study? This shift in emphasis prepares the ground for detailed descriptions of how "we" (not the electronic devices) immediately experience space, time, and consequence.

In *Introduction to the Human Sciences (1883),* Wilhelm Dilthey observed that the natural sciences use abstraction and measurement to a degree that would be unacceptable in the human sciences. Ghost research, as a form of inquiry that deals with the possibility of a human afterlife, must involve itself with human experience, not electronic measurement, as simply recording a distinction between what is now and what actually happened a moment or a measured time ago. Ghost research is not measured time. It is exploring the past as a mode of present experience:

"A fixed and finished past....is a past divorced from evidence....and is consequently nothing and unknowable; it must belong to the present world of experience" (Oakeshott 1933: 107).

And the use, in "ghost hunting" and "paranormal investigations", of saturating a haunted location with an arsenal of technology is not (in most instances) being contextual to the past productions of that site. And, its use to analyze what's going on at the location is <u>not</u> a bow to science or a nod to the scientific community.

It IS demonstrating: "Hey look. We are doing scientific investigations". This is "technophilia". It is the current trend, a TV "ghost hunting" trope, on the part of the paranormal community, to throw (and show) the latest and "best" technology at a haunted site to generate something – anything – that might stir interest in their work. This is not "leaping the fence". It is the process of becoming "weighed down" with technology so much so that you <u>can't</u> leap it!

And this "ghost hunting" trope has consequences:

"An action repeated again and again and again, however fractured or partial or incomplete, has a kind of staying power – persists through time... (Schneider 2013:37).

That persistence, enacted in a "ghost hunt" and on "ghost tours", using "demand and command" tactics and a mediating technology, simply adds another contemporary layer of presence. It does not "unearth" or document what haunts us from the past. It creates a haunting future presence!

Also, if we perform as 21st c. individuals, we lose our intended past identity, an essential quality needed to socially relate, and entangle ourselves with any remaining past presences. More importantly, we negate a non-intrusive immersion into the past. This non-intrusion is a "prime directive" of a "ghost excavation"!

21st c. "hunting" tactics, using intrusive contemporary technology, to entice (or document) a "manifestation", can confuse <u>and</u> be harmful. In the same vein, Carl Sagan once asked if we are:

"interfering with the scheme of causality (that) **has led to our own time and to ourselves".**

The concept of "leaping the fence" by unbounding the subject matter (in our case, a "haunting") and object inquiry (our "ghostly presence") is not new. It is part of a tradition of post-humanist scholarship (cf. Butler

1993), and has historical roots in both anthropology and archaeology (cf. Kirk 2006; Fowler 2013).

In a "ghost excavation", we are not "interfering" with the past by merely "witnessing" or participating in <u>their</u> experiences. But what happens when we teach them, or show them, something "new"? Does <u>that</u> entanglement have future consequences?

We need to view this haunted landscape as enveloped in cultural processes that still continue, and not confine it to physical measurements. These measurements define and build "fences". We must leap these "fences" to broaden our vision of what lies, not only within, but also beneath, hidden in layers, on the surface. This "leap" is <u>not</u> a "leap of faith", based on a firm belief that a particular place (or landscape) is "haunted" by "ghosts". This "leap" is accomplished through performance practices.

Barthes (1977) defines landscapes as a system of "signs" and symbols ("signifiers"). These are cultural in nature, not deviations on a meter. In this way, a landscape, albeit a "haunted" one, can be "read" within a cultural construct, not a "paranormal" one.

These cultural symbols are a palimpsest of cultural practices and beliefs that occur as "pages" or layers of memory occupying the spaces of a landscape. They are not "fenced-in" by horizontal or vertical boundaries, such as the current popular trope ("ghost hunting" or "paranormal investigation"), or even the limitations set by the reality of contemporary thought, academia, and science.

Michael Conzen (1994) summarizes this layering as one means to analyze what remains:

"to view the landscape historically is to acknowledge its cumulative character, to acknowledge that nature, symbolism, and design are not static elements of the human record but change with historical experience...." (1994: 4).

We cannot measure environmental deviation when we don't acknowledge a fluctuating "baseline" of previous layers of potentially different "readings". This is because the emphasis of "ghost hunting" (or "paranormal investigation") is horizontal physical deviation, without a consideration of the vertical cultural agency (and physical residual readings) of variability that may remain in a "haunted" (or any other) landscape setting.

"Nowadays, when I pass along the walk where the tenements were leveled, I persist in seeing, not the

massive architecture of the new building, but the dust and the stones where, in my mind, the dogs still lie in the October wind"

- **Loren Eiseley, in** *All the Strange Hours: The Excavation of a Life (1975).*

This is the vision, the altered state of perception, I want to envision for ghost research. It is something that lies beyond the horizontal plane, the contemporary measurement of space, and the current dimensions of scientific reality:

"I look upon this great building….I see right through it to the bare field left by the demolition of the slum. Something has seized and held me there, created what is even more real than what currently exists" (Eiseley 1975: 150).

This perceived vertical dimension on the surface is my haunted space. It is where I dig. It is an alternative, altering state of what remains from the past. It is a vision that is largely absent from ghost research as it is currently performed in "ghost hunts" and "paranormal investigation".

During a "ghost excavation", our sense of place, as some particular place distinctively past, is never displaced. It replaces the current modality. It jumps the fence. We remain in character because fragments of that past (perhaps multiple pasts) still remain, present. A displacement of time is not felt. We continue our intended "identity" to the past because this identity allows communication with that past to flow.

This character emplacement in (with) the past, during a "ghost excavation", and without concerning ourselves with contemporary environmental scans (which displace our identity), reinforces our sense (and experience) of a connection we make ("unearth") to what happened (is happening) at haunted locations.

The here and now is not sensed or apprehended as reminders (and remainders) of the past. We must "dig" deep to immerse ourselves, remaining there throughout the "excavation" process. In a similar sense, the past (as a particular episode of a specific past), as residual and/or active presence, remains attached as a "haunting" to a past space and a sense of being (as something experienced and remembered in memory).

At the precise moment of contact (an immersive scenario that produces an intentional manifestation), inscribing a context and time, is when perceptions unfold. At this moment, a "border" has been crossed, and the arbitrary fence separating past and present (and dead/buried; alive/interacting) has been "jumped". During this moment of manifestation, a "haunting" becoming present, space, time, and reality start to change. Awareness has shifted, and although <u>not</u> a "paranormal" event, the character of the space is now transformed back to a past and active situation.

This is place-making. It is not place measurement. It is the past becoming present. It is not this present place as "haunted" by "ghosts". It is a more common experience: this happened here....and what still remains are "S.C.A.R.S." (**S**trata **C**ontext **A**ssociations of **R**emains in **S**pace) of past productions (and occupations) of that space. The "ghost" is a metaphor for something uncanny, ephemeral, and transient. A "S.C.A.R." is "what" and "who" continues to be present, as remains from the past. This place-making, as an "excavation tool" (the contextual scenario) is part of the archaeological imagination.

A "ghost excavation" is remembering what happened here, which provides a baseline for imagining what might remain. It delimits a workable field of possibilities. Performances of these contextual cultural scenarios provide "cues" to invoke (not provoke) "clues" of what remains. This produces a different and expanded vision of what might remain from the historical and cultural record of what occurred in that space in the past. It opens the possibility whereby portions of that past, once thought dead and buried, are brought once again into being.

This "becoming present", through digging-deep and <u>then</u> "excavating" the possibilities, is a means of expanding and revising history. Excavation is a means to explore not merely how things might have been sensed and experienced, but also how the (a) past might have been different from what prior research (and historical narrative) had supposed. The exploratory exercise of "excavation performances" is a regular social process, not a "paranormal" one. It is straightforward, and is not couched in (or framed by) metaphysical "fences".

This place-making, or "unearthing", what "haunts" a place still, is a form of cultural activity. It is not a measurement of space. It requires ethnographic sensitivity, not precise and measured devices. What may manifest can only be grasped in relation to the ideas, behaviors, and performances with which a manifestation becomes present. And the nature of the manifestation (its intention) must be understood by means of ethnographic knowledge: the past cultural world where and when it was produced. Knowledge of

<u>that</u> world is essential, and is <u>not</u> a measurement of this present one.

Ghost Research: The "Mess"

There is a mess in ghost research today! This mess is not the fault of "ghost hunting", paranormal reality TV, ghost tourism, para-celebrity events, or fieldwork as entertainment. Ghosts and hauntings do not have much form at all. They appear and disappear. They are unpredictable. If much of this "haunted" world is unclear, non-specific, emotional, ephemeral, and elusive, then where does the science of it enter? How might we document and record more of this reality? Could we "know" these ghosts better? Should we?

To begin is to think anew. If reality is not a law of science, if some of it is elusive and ephemeral, if it seems messy, then the fieldwork to document this reality is not a simple field of entertainment, a simple command, or a measurement on an electronic device! The reality of what this "other" world of reality entails is that we're going to have to re-teach ourselves to think, to perform differently, to better relate to these "others" in a different <u>social</u> manner (not electronically or as a form that entertains or scares), and to know these "others" in new ways.

A haunting is a matter (and a form) that moves: from a "dead end" to a continuing presence as cultural practice. This is a voyage from death back into life. In this sense, the past becomes a multiplicity of real possibilities (rather than ruin), expanding our concept (not "fencing-in") of contemporary reality.

Ghost research is an exploratory trope. The mapping of past worlds is still incomplete, though contemporary maps indicate "terra incognito". In our explorations, we must penetrate and expose the mythologies of misinformation that build-up through the entertainment media of TV "ghost hunting". Society builds popular accounts around this entertainment which often obscures what remains from the past.

One way (of perhaps many) to understand the reality of a haunting, what and who remains from a past once thought dead and buried, is through our bodies: an immersive embodiment. This is "becoming", in some particular way, a part of their world, and identified as such. Knowing them, in this example, is becoming an "insider", not an "outsider" with different clothing, objects, and ways of expression that don't fit the context of that past world, or that past situation, or that act in the past.

Photo 2: The "team" preparing for a "Ghost Excavation"

These are performance practices, an understanding of the poetics (not the horror or thrill) of a haunting. The "ghost excavation" is a narrative of intervention, and one means to communicate with the "Other" on their terms (as an ethnography of communication or "E.O.C."), not a contemporary "ghost hunting" one ("command and demand"). This is intimacy that is not based on a close physical proximity to them.

We must not limit our understanding of the world and reality by making it "paranormal". Research methods, to be accepted as science, cannot be allowed to claim a monopoly on a particular mode of execution, i.e. research <u>must</u> be done a certain way to be acceptable. This restricted way of thinking constrains research. It creates a certain vision that binds and blinds us to other ways of knowing!

We must now allow the "commandments" or commands of contemporary science to dictate how we "see", "think", "imagine", and what we must do when we investigate. This is especially true with the overuse of statistical sampling. As John Law (2004) suggests, these rules and practices **"not only describe, but also help to produce the reality that they understand" (2004: 5).**

This type of scientific thinking and doing – what is important, what information we need to gather, how we should collect it – has become institutionalized as the "common sense" of doing research and fieldwork. Yet, this line of reasoning, this "scientific method", works on the assumption **"that the world is properly to be understood as a set of fairly specific, determinate, and more or less identifiable processes" (Law 2004: 5).** Is it?

This scientific approach is a framing device, a builder of fences. Research, fieldwork, arguments, and data about reality must take place within this arena of knowing. And that is the problem! That's why these same scientists label ghost research, in all its manifestations, a fringe pseudo-science, at best!

This is because for them, these "academic tribes", ghost research lies outside the "territory" of the scientific frame of doing research and fieldwork, out there on the fringes. The task before us is to imagine research and methods where we can <u>also</u> seek those "Others". This involves, I propose, an altered state in both our ways of thinking and our means of doing research and fieldwork!

A haunting is not simply just a paranormal event because the past becoming present is difficult to understand, technically out of reach the vast majority of the time. Is it? Regularities and repetitions, as law-like generalizations, what science strives for, sets limitations. Should an exploration of possibilities set these limitations?

The need is for variation, not conformity. To acknowledge a haunting is a way of opening space for the ephemeral in reality. It is another image of the world, a different kind of experience (attainable and understandable), and something that is <u>not</u> beyond our limits to document and record, albeit in a non-conventional but still humanly possible manner.

What this means in research, in development, and in practice out there in the field, is to explore what Law (2004) calls **"methods assemblages" (2004: 14):**

"enactments of relations that make some things….present….whilst making others absent 'out there'" (Ibid: 14).

Most "ghost hunts" are a "mess" that largely makes absence. Paranormal investigation, as a bow to contemporary science, is limiting in the same sense. It is an attempt at a framing device to suit a hoped for scientific scrutiny and acceptance.

A "ghost excavation" is one example of this "methods assemblage". It uses contextual performance practices (as "enactments") to embed oneself in particular situations of the past. It is, to use Law's phrasing, an example of **"a combination of reality detector and reality amplifier" (2004: 14).** Performance is a tool, not an electronic device. It detects a presence becoming present by "amplifying", through performance practices, the memories of what behaviors and experiences might have occurred in the past in particular acts, situations, and events (both emotional and mundane) within particular historically-known individual biographies.

Reality is not a certainty. It is a social practice. What happened in the past and what remains today, is not always dead and passive (or in ruin). It is also not something that is waiting to be excavated by archaeologists, viewed by ethnographers, or recorded and measured by paranormal investigators.

There must be a social and sociable interchange between two or more interested parties. Ghost research is not about academic politics, entertaining economics, or ego/prestige enhancement. It is about re-connecting to social reality. As meddlers of time and presence, "ghost hunters" must take active responsibility into the exploration of a haunting. That they must should go without saying. That they do is a different matter. As Boyd (2002) states:

"The time has surely come to fulfill our obligations to the people of the past, the present, and the future, and to increase those possibilities beyond the narrow confines of academic practice" (2002:36).

Perhaps, the model that we need is that of **"partial connection" (Strathern 1991)** back to understanding past sociability? Law (2004) states:

"We need to find ways of elaborating quiet methods, slow methods, or modest methods. In particular, we need to discover ways of making methods without accompanying imperialisms" (2004: 15).

We need to do ghost research without attaching politics or a form of personal entertainment to the social equation!

Para-History as a "Haunting"

In today's world of ghost tourism, there is "edutainment": a little dash of history, a lot more hint of a hyper-entertaining experience. Where does the difference lie between contextual authenticity and a theatrical ghosting of a horrific event: between the horrors of a former Civil War battlefield, and the "edutainment" of a "ghost tour" on that battlefield?

Ghost tourism looks for authentic sensations and experiences without worrying itself about problems of archaeology (layers of memory), anthropology (cultural context) or historical (meaningful behavioral) authenticity. Even its "staged authenticity" is not attentive to the quality of the "copy". A "feeling" of authenticity is enough, not its legitimacy! A "taste" of history suffices, but not enough to spoil the experience.

What does count is a good memory, not necessarily a real one. When one distances oneself from authenticity, one inevitably enters a pseudo-para world of contrivance, misrepresentation, and deceit. Sometimes, there is even conceit towards what really happened in the past because the history was not entertaining (or horrific) enough!

On these ghost tours, what is important is not the authenticity of the past event, but the authenticity of a contemporary experience, gaining strength from its "repeatability" for each group of public listeners and observers. The "ghostly" manifestation becomes a "captive" performer, not a real historical figure locked in a tragedy. These tours re-invent the reality of historical narrative. They become "para-history".

Ghost tourism, and most "ghost hunts", is an example of "short memory", not historical memory. It is a feature of contemporary culture, constructed with the pace and tempo of internet entertainment. It is a commitment to rapid change, superficial obligations, updating trends, and keeping in touch with "pop culture". "Ghost hunting" is continually offering new devices, new reality shows, and new locations where one can "hunt" ghosts.

Ghost tourism is an essential, albeit economic, part of the new post-modern reality trope characterized by:

- Nocturnal activity and experiential use of "trending" locations;
- An "excitable", entertaining, and superficial "gaze";
- The pleasure of using "disguise" rather than authenticity;
- Little historical and ethnographic evocation;
- Themed activities and devices; and
- Attention to sensorial details, rather than controlled and contextual executions.

This is not science. It is "edutainment". Ghost tourism (or "ghost hunting") is not cultural exploration or ethnographic fieldwork. It is emotional tourism. The "atmosphere" of a place is more sought after than its true ethno-history. This does not expand reality. It builds walls around (and encloses) present un-reality.

This "short memory" (before something new comes along) is tied to an eternal present story, while the real context (ethno-history) is not "entertained" as a real presence of the past in the present. This ethno-historical context should be the "home" of ghost research, changing to different cultural contexts and site history as we explore each haunted location. Ghost research must become a "home", grounded in historic memory-making practices, not ones continuously repeated as "para-present".

Thick Description: More Important Than Tech Thickness in Ghost Research

"There is no such thing as a human nature without culture"

- **Clifford Geertz, Anthropologist.**

Clifford Geertz was an advocate of an interpretive anthropology based on "thick description". This involved detailed research, writing, and performances in the field that communicated the role of culture as a context within which particular actions become meaningful. These specific actions, by allowing a particular identity and cultural resonance to emerge, open a way to **"the imaginative universe within which their acts are signs" (Geertz 1973:13).**

During fieldwork, ethnographers participate in the local culture in such a way as to make their behavior both meaningful (to the people they are studying) and appropriate to the culture in which that fieldwork takes place. The anthropologist, as participant-observer, is like an actor, learning and performing particular "roles", and using appropriate behaviors that are essential to the social context that is being explored. Anthropologist Colin Turnbull writes:

"….we have to present….in such a manner as to be comprehensible and (I hope) significant to others" (1979:3).

We must do, I propose, this same type of performance, as a "thick description", in ghost research. This becomes more than a study of a haunting (or its "debunking") at a particular location in a specific space. It goes beyond a tech sweep of space. It becomes an immersion into the "mindscape" of past cultural beings, not "paranormal" entities. This immersion, and its identification and acceptance by a culturally-ghostly presence, is achieved by this "thick" performance. It cannot be achieved by a contemporary profile and the use of "out of context" tech devices.

A "thick" performance becomes an exploration of past cultural worlds, not contemporary measured spaces. It becomes an immersion into past cultural beliefs and expressions of past semiotic systems ("signs"), not present-day beliefs or individual/group peer pressure to "do it like they do it on TV".

This "thick" immersion involves the development of "thick" situational scenarios, based in researching the multiple past productions of spaces of particular locations and intra-site spaces: **This Happened Here!** The use of the past tense establishes cultural context for the situational "thick" scenarios. This is an attempt, during the fieldwork, to embody as much verisimilitude as possible with respect to the past culture and "attached" individuals in which a particular haunting is hypothesized to be occurring.

The situational scenarios form a cultural baseline, a "sounding board" as it were.

Photo 3: The Enactment of a "Thick" Situational Scenario

It sets the investigator as a character in a haunted mise-en-scene, an individual that can be identified as performing particular (and appropriate) cultural behaviors. The enactment of these situational scenarios forces us to concentrate our listening and observations on particular <u>appropriate</u> (and contextual) outcomes.

This becomes a **"precissing".** This is, as used by anthropologist Bilinda Straight (2007) in an ethnographic study of extraordinary experience among the Samburu on Northern Kenya:

"the process by which we reduce the potentially infinite we are in contact with in world to the cognizably finite...(2007:15).

A manifestation, in the context of an enacted performance "targeting" a particular past situation that occurred in that particular space, becomes a particular past presence responding to that performance. It reduces the natural or coincidence to what a person (as "ghost") would (should) do and/or say.

This is documenting a cultural process of "entanglement", a relationship of becoming present in contemporary reality. It is not a description of one's inner thoughts or feelings. This is an "excavation" that produces this "entanglement" of what (and perhaps "who") still remains. It is not a random "hunt", an environmental scan, or a "debunking" of previous (perhaps non-contextual) experiences.

Using a "thick description" to process a haunting in the field (and not afterward in a hotel room or at home) helps us to experience the human entangled nature of a haunting, and not its assumed "paranormal" tone. This views a haunting as a field of potentiality, in which many cultural scenarios are possible but are reduced by the "precissing" of the performance "excavation" practices.

Note:

A "ghost excavation" is fieldwork that is <u>not</u> meant for private, still occupied residences. This is archaeological work, and as such it deals with permanently unoccupied, ruined, and/or abandoned sites. These are our haunted "stages" where we work and "excavate".

On Ownership and Present Politics

There is a long-standing belief in the paranormal community that a site in ruin, or abandoned, does not retain any <u>past</u> ownership. After all, those who resided there, worked there, are now dead and buried. Right? But an exploration of these places, these sites that appear "haunted", even with present distant ownership approval, may represent a form of "trespass" into the lives and "homes" of "others".

This raises certain ethical and moral issues, especially with the behavior and attitude of some "ghost hunting" groups. It also invokes important concerns regarding social boundaries, occurring between what is "public" and "private", in relation to these "hunts'/investigations.

What is even more dubious are the claims of certain groups and/or individuals today who regard these sites as their "own" private "hunting ground"! Is this a form of exclusive contemporary "territoriality"? Do these individuals or groups have that right, at the expense of those who may remain?

Instead of seeking "permission" of those who may remain from the past, why must one seek "admission" from a contemporary "ghost hunting" group? Who are the real "ghosts" of these haunted sites? Is it those who come to "hunt" for a short period, or those who still remain in residence there? Who becomes the "host": the "ghost hunter" or the "lingering resident"?

Why "Excavating" the Elusive and Ephemeral "Haunts" Us and the Future

Do the possibility of continuing social dimensions and historical contexts, as past "entanglements", count as worthy objects of study in ghost research? I propose that they do because they must be considered an integral component of the archaeological record, and contemporary reality, of a haunted site. Some past "entanglements" continue as present manifesting assemblages.

These remains, theoretically, must include all past acts, social exchanges, and situations/events that occurred in a particular space in the past <u>and</u> recorded in historical and ethnographic narratives. A more radical concept of possible remains would include past beliefs, memories, and sensory experiences that would have occurred, and have become embedded (or "attached") in various spaces of a haunted location.

The basic question <u>every</u> investigator of haunted space should ask is whether one is recovering the past in this fieldwork, or is one creating an alternative future history for the site. The process of data gathering must be objective, rigorous in detail, systematic, contextual and performance-based. If not, fieldwork remains a "hunt", yet staying within the bounds of conventionality. Because of this, without any entanglement to past productions of space, contemporary fieldwork itself becomes a production of new layers in future tense!

Let's change that attitude and behavioral stance. Let's step over this conventionality of "ghost hunting" and "paranormal investigating". Let's begin with research....

Research

A. Introduction

In any location (or landscape setting), individual and group social and habitual practices, operating in the company of particular cultural codes, were performed. At a haunted location, some of these past behavioral practices continue. It is up to the investigator to "crack the (cultural) code" of the haunting: what remains of these cultural practices in particular a space.

The ability to document and record a past presence requires a situated competency in past cultural contexts and situations. This competency must lie at the center of contemporary ghost research. And it begins with ethno-historical research.

B. Authenticity in Research and Exhibition

Today, there is a mass "mess" of popular culture venues and "exhibits" which attempt to demonstrate the world of the paranormal to contemporary society. Is this really the reality of past presence remaining today at haunted locations? Are these examples of data as evidence or entertainment, or a combination of both? Do they help or hinder legitimate (or serious) research? What research and "displays" of presence is considered more respectable? Does fieldwork become more respectable when one sticks to the facts of past history, cultural practices, and biographical information?

What use is an entertaining experience in this search for the reality of presence? What is the value of knowledge in an entertainment context? Perhaps, value becomes an exchange value? What can an investigator obtain by following this entertaining perspective? This becomes something which means something to someone today, not something relevant for someone who may remain from the past! The entertainment mode is a "tool", but it is not a tool of legitimate research, in any field of serious inquiry.

As an archaeologist, I gather data from the field according to an archaeological purpose: the recovery of what (be it material, sensory, residual, or interactive) remains from the past. In my fieldwork, and the subsequent "exhibition" of data (books, website, lectures), I am exercising a choice in selecting and gathering together this "exhibit". It is about a concerned desire to demonstrate what comes from fieldwork based on the recovery of remains through an ethno-archaeological context, not some form of entertainment.

The context and cultural value of a recorded manifestation becoming present depends upon how it is recovered. If one mixes a surface walk-thru, an unattended and unperformed electronic device, an instrument scan, a notion of entertainment, or a use of present tense ("I am....."; Is anyone here?"; "Make something happen!"), then a manifestation (in any sensory modality) is of little use in producing any ethno-historical data of a past presence in contemporary reality. This is because there is no basis for an entanglement with the past through the establishment of both identity and a social relationship.

A proper (and respectful) relative mix of resonating acts must have as its primary purpose "sociability", not entertainment or measurement. The power of "attraction" (as social entanglement) is about signification: something that is meaningful to a particular individual or individuals from the past.

A sincere, and personal, human exchange is, I propose, the vital "energy" necessary for a manifestation to occur. This "energy" is based on identity and intent coming together. We (the investigative team) are identified in a positive way by our actions, and they (the "ghosts") respond to that identity. That is a social entanglement with the past, and is similar to how it might have occurred in a particular historical moment and cultural situation.

Photo 4: The Moment of "Entanglement" in a "Ghost Excavation"

C. Cultural Relevance in Ghost Research

Forget the tech tools, ignore the belief system engrained in "ghost hunting", step away from the pseudo-science nonsense reported (so often) as "paranormal investigation", and experience, through an immersed entanglement, what really remains of the past at haunted locations! There is more to the world of a haunting than "I think, therefore they are". Being or becoming present is more than a "beep" or measurement away. It is a relationship based on identity. It is a social entanglement between past and contemporary presences.

In our research, we must first turn to anthropology, not physics, to enrich (and "en-liven") ghost research. As Jeremy Trombley asserts:

"Anthropology becomes a practice, not merely of understanding others, but of constructing a world of relations with others….one that behaves as if the world is not given, that recognizes the presence and active participation of all kinds of beings…." (2012:3-4).

We must replace the technological detachment used in the field to promote a "scientific" investigation. These tools do not replace experience and social entanglement. They do not engage "who" may remain. Often, they do the opposite: they disengage any type of potential social relationship. Is it any wonder there is often heard "get out" (or something similar) on audio recordings?

We must participate in acts and practices that are rich in symbolism and meaning for past (potential) audiences. Ghost research must become ethnography of performance, and not an applied technology that distances us from them. This engagement with the past is not about being culturally relative so much as it is being culturally relevant.

D. The "Afterlife" of Historical Texts: Using Experience that Counts in Research

In our research, before entering the field, we must go beyond the written narrative as mere descriptive text. If the written word is **"held to be the primary distinguishing feature of humanity" (Tilley 1991:16)**, then it is the archaeologist (in fieldwork at haunted locations) that elevates words to a level beyond their historical use into a discussion of texts as contextual "artifacts" in their own right (Moreland 2001).

What is the stratum of memory of words in historical narratives that provides us with "cues" and "clues" of the cultural experience, and social entanglements, of particular situations and specific events in the past? When, to what extent, and to whom were the documents written? As Ian Hodder (1998) states: **"what people say"** is often very different from **"what people do (1998:113).**

According to Danet (1997), books carry traces of **"the history of the hands that have touched them" (1997:9).** This entanglement goes beyond "object animation" or a "haunted object". Words represent individual experience. In these texts, a physical setting is located, and there hints at the structure of cultural life. A relationship, the past entanglement, occurs between place, space, memory, belief, life, and things (material and sensory culture). This remains embedded in the text and, some of it, is embedded in the spaces of a haunted location.

Conceiving of the historical narrative as material reality of the past enables us to construct a biography of the entanglement. With it, we can explore its potential "afterlife" as a potential haunting "cue" <u>and</u> a "clue" to what remains from the past (and continues to manifest). The modern English word "experiment" best preserves the original meaning of "experience" (Desjarlais 1996:73). In a "ghost excavation", we experiment with performance entanglements (as "cues") in order to get "clues" about what is manifesting at these haunted locations.

Unearthing the meaning beneath the text in historical narratives is an experiment into past experience. We take this research to the field and design our "excavation" around these narratives. This provides us with a relationship (an entanglement) between field experiments (the performance practices) and what we experience (the "clues") in the field.

The experiments that we conduct with contextual performance practices (as enacted cultural scenarios) become an external engagement, a social entanglement between "like" minds. It is a haunting experience with one's surroundings (in particular spaces) and focuses on what remains from the past at haunted locations.

However, an experienced sense of presence can incur a multitude of meanings. The performance practices (as "cues" framed as cultural scenarios) have the function of a controlling mechanism: it "targets" a particular meaning as a "clue" to what remains. A particular meaning becomes present ("manifests"; is "unearthed"), which is attached to an intentional response that is contextual to particular historical narratives. And this is the "clue" that identifies past experiential moments in particular situations (or during specific events).

Heidegger (1971) writes:

"to experience is to go along a way. The way leads through a landscape" (1971:67).

That landscape, in a "ghost excavation", is organized into particular layers of past memories, temporally and spatially framed. They are based on ethno-historical texts of what happened, and how life was lived, in particular landscape settings. These texts are critical research tools in an "excavation" at haunted locations. The task of a "ghost excavation" is to use these research tools to identify where, when, and why people experience a manifestation at these locations, and the conditions (the entangled performance practices) that makes the process possible.

E. A Research Example: The "Culture of War"

Exploring cultural manifestations at haunted locations requires a nod to, and knowledge of, those concepts, practices, emotions, and experiences from a particular past, and a specific past culture that:

- Have long histories of occupation, and that are not temporary, "pop culture" manifestations; and
- Individuals actively occupy them in participatory, often emotional, traumatic situations.

One particular past is the period of the American Civil War. One specific culture of that period is the "culture of war" and its entanglement with the "culture of death" of that time (cf. Sabol 2014).

Military campaigns do more than elaborate casualty lists and destroy property and landscapes. They also create cultural order: symbols, behavioral patterns, and signals. A battlefield is an example of this cultural order (the "culture of war"). Battle or combat is a socio-cultural act, a ritual performed with rules, obligations, expectations, and survival concerns.

These were reinforced by drills and the military culture "soundmarks" (bugle calls; drumming; officer commands). This created an ordered Inherent Military Probability or I.M.P., for the most part, on American Civil War battlefields. It is how the soldier should (would) have acted, and what he (sometimes she) would have experienced in combat.

Two meaningful events occurred on a Civil War battlefield: protection/movement and survival/death. Both produced subsequent "signs" of these events, and created layers of memory and cultural transmission. First, order was governed by the "culture of war" protocols inherited from previous campaigns and wars. These involved separate military stages:

- Rules of drill;
- Rules of signals/signs; and
- Rules of space (the K.O.C.O.A. military terrain).

Second, the battlefield experience, based on particular socio-cultural beliefs (the "culture of death"), created a life of remembrance (if one survived) or, I propose, a potential "afterlife" of cultural memories.

According to Barth (1987):

"Ritual activity (such as military behavior of a particular "culture of war") **frequently involve a practical**

remembering effected through the experience and manifestation of symbolic material items" (1987:75).

For the survivors of battles and war, this is reflected in war memorialization, reunions, and heritage events. But the dead who may remain (as "ghosts"), aspects of this military order continue to manifest today as elements of residual traces and afterlife conscious memory traces.

What may survive, remain, and manifest (as part of an ethno-archaeological record), must be, I propose, must be **"in some way related to social realities" (cf. Hodder 1978).** The potential for the manifestation of these traces must be related, I suggest, to the belief system of the soldier at the time of death. During the American Civil War, I have proposed (Sabol 2014) that the reason why some of these Civil War battlefields are haunted by past presence is because of this belief in a particular "culture of death": dying the "good death".

I utilize this data about the "culture of war" and the "culture of death" to develop contextual scenarios that we used in "ghost excavations" on these Civil War battlefields. We do this in order to entangle our performances with similar acts (and experiences) a soldier would have had (and perhaps still recalls in memory). This is meant to create a relational sociability between us and specific past presences (for more information on this relational archaeological approach and its effect on social entanglement see below).

Photo 5: A Battlefield "Ghost Excavation"

Fieldwork

A. <u>Re-Constructing the Haunted Location</u>

How should we perceive and document the past at a haunted location? How can we construct knowledge from ephemeral and trace presences? We must begin with practices that had meaning in the past. We must appreciate that some remains that manifest (are "unearthed") form part of a past social world that is still present.

We must also avoid any strict adherence to how this type of fieldwork should evolve as sensory remains begin to be "unearthed" and manifest. We must, however, involve ourselves with social re-construction at these sites, putting remains into past (not present) <u>cultural</u> context. We must devise means and tools which enable us to be both sensitive to this potential sociability and be ethical in the process.

By definition, the past cannot be present. That it is, and we see it all around us (besides at haunted locations), is obvious. <u>A</u> past has been completed, but other vestiges, traces, and remains of particular, some biographical, elements of the (perhaps multiple) past(s) still exist today. This is reality, albeit archaeological reality. Archaeological work recovers the past in the present. But that is not all. A ruin, without archaeological intervention, is also a past presence. And so is a haunted location.

Ghost research, like archaeology, must not be mere observational work: observe what is "excavated" or what the instruments are measuring, the monitor is displaying, or the audio is recording. It must become, first, a participatory practice. We must perform to observe what may be left of the past in particular spaces.

This participatory/performance stance, however, must not be reduced to the status of mere contemporary entertainment, as a spectacle of excess. It must be contextual, remaining rooted to an event, situation, or act in the past, and/or a particular biographical episode of a particular individual (known to have once occupied that space).

This is a focus on social entanglements, relative to what occurred at particular locations and specific spaces in the past, perhaps multiple pasts. This is the basic premise of a "ghost excavation" at a haunted location.

B. <u>T.E.A.M. Concept</u>

Haunted space is an inter-relational entanglement of fieldwork that includes:

- **T.** = Theatrical empathy (character building; establishment of a particular past identity);
- **E.** = Ethnographic sensitivity (using techniques that analyze human culture);
- **A.** = Archaeological sensibility (dealing with multiple layers of memory as trace residuals and interactive fragments of social behaviors); and
- **M.** = Management (forensics: using "cues" to determine "clues"= what or "who" remains after an ethno-historical event, act, or situation).

The T.E.A.M. concept is a social entanglement between a non-intrusive methodology and documentary-recording devices without technological overload. It deals with past human behaviors, not the measurements of contemporary space. It is not a "hunt". It is a performance "excavation".

Haunted space is an inter-relational landscape. It combines archaeological (layers of memory), ethnographic (cultural ritual and behavior), and theatrical (actors and situational poses) components. A "ghost excavation" is work in a particular setting (as a theatrical stage), involving performances ("excavation"), aimed at a specific audience ("ghostly" presence). The "excavation" involves an entanglement between depth (the past) and surface (contemporary manifestations in the present).

In a "ghost excavation, we are not searching for something that is "paranormal". We are also not attempting to "debunk" past subjective experiences. We are attempting to "unearth" the "S.C.A.R.S." left from the past. We are interested in those "S.C.A.R.S.", as traces and presences of continued past human activity.

C. <u>The S.C.A.R. of a Haunting</u>

An intentional, interactive manifestation and communication (as opposed to a residual) does not occur in a vacuum, a space without socio-cultural significance. A "ghost" is not simply a "ghost". He/she is a cultural being. A haunting is framed by participants, setting, and appropriate channels of social behavior that are place-making entanglements.

A haunting is composed of a socio-cultural entanglement of elements relative to a particular occupation of space. This is what (and sometimes) "who" remains. This entanglement constitutes a "s.c.a.r." from the past:

- **S.** = The setting (space) of a particular past event, or act in history;
- **C.** = The context, involving the social parameters of that event or act;
- **A.** = The association, which is the accompanying signs or symbols (sensory elements) of that event or act; and
- **R.** = The remnants of what are left, framed as a social interaction (assemblage) from a particular strata of memory in history.

In summary, a haunting is a layer of memory of socio-historical context that is associated with specific remains that occur in particular spaces at a haunted location. These assemblages of remains are **"actants" (Latour 1993).** This is anything (and anyone) that leaves a trace in the unfolding of a situated event. These "actants" cause something to happen. In certain locations, their manifesting presence ("s.c.a.r.") is perceived to be a "haunting" from the past.

D. Haunting Manifestations ("S.C.A.R."): Are They Intentional and Dialogic?

It has become quite customary (a "haunting" itself) in "ghost hunting" and "paranormal investigation" to use certain verbal expressions. These verbal expressions (such as "Is anyone her with us tonight?"; "Can you... (do something?") usually increases with the amount of technology one uses during an exploration of a haunted location. But what about the "manifestations" that occur during these verbal "demands and commands"? Are they intentional responses from an afterlife conscious mind, an unintentional projection confirming projection of an investigator's hoped-for response, a habitual response from a "trigger" stimulus from an un-thinking ("brainless") entity, or none of the above?

A "manifestation", above all must be dialogical. This is both a coordinating effort of individual actions ("intentional"), and the actions of one person making possible the actions of another. There is a relation, albeit social, between two beings that entangle them in a socially-constructed situational dialogue.

In essence, what this means, I propose, is that in haunted space, it is the investigator's actions (their particular performance), accommodating past socially-prescribed rules and identity, that creates this social entanglement between what is past (but present) and the contemporary situation (an "excavation"). It is <u>not</u> because a required action is imposed on the other ("do something"). The particular performance practice(s) of the investigator relates to, and is in a socially-acceptable cadence, I propose, with the social practices of the "other" (the "ghost"). This creates the entanglement, the same (or sufficiently similar) positions in a social field of relations.

An investigator should feel this "cadence experience" (entanglement) becoming present through actions, and not command it to happen, or hope that it will occur. It becomes an understanding of the "haunting" (or entanglement) sensually, so that when one participates with the manifesting presence (not document it "after the fact" in a "reveal"), it is in dialogue with the patterns of past practices known to have occurred at the location.

These manifestations should directly relate to the patterns of past practices, as part of social conventionality <u>then</u> (not today). And this makes sense to us now (and not perceived as a "paranormal" event). This is because we have researched those social conventions prior to investigating the site.

The use of disciplinary power (and an attempt at control), such as the commands to "show us a sign" and "do something" may not work, or be received well, in other (past) social situations. Is it any wonder "ghost hunters" get EVP recordings of "Get Out!", and/or physical contact ("pushing" and "shoving")?

These manifestations are not demonic. They are socio-cultural, embedded in past customs and cultural protocols of sociability!

Note: In some cultures (the "culture of war"), spaces (battlefields), and situations (combat), demands and commands would be deemed appropriate.

A "ghost excavation" uses the concept of "citationality" as a fieldwork practice. This holds that our actions are not intelligible, therefore not affective (for the most part except for "get out"), unless they relate to the norms and practices set by previous social customs, such as those of the past culture under study.

This does not mean "duplicating" them, as it a "re-enactment" (see below), but "citing" it in a way that makes sense to particular past presences. This is what we do in a "ghost excavation", through the use of "P.O.P.":

- We "perform" past situations without "duplicating" them;
- We "observe" what happens (if anything); and
- We "participate" in/with what ("who") manifests.

P.O.P. is important because it is a relational model. In this model, for an entanglement to occur, identity becomes extremely important. One's (past) identity is created during the performance practices (the investigator as past actor), and in intentional manifestations to those performance practices (the past actor as manifesting presence).

Relationships are not given (pre-established). They form, becoming an entanglement, as we shift from task to task (cf. Ingold 200), and one performance to another in a "ghost excavation":

"It is not by their inner attributes that persons are identified, but by their positions vis-à-vis one another in the relational field" (Ingold 2000: 149).

Occupying a particular position in a past relational field requires finding a dialogical rhythm with the occupants of this field (Ingold 2000: 353). We accomplish this through ethno-historical research (mentioned above). This is examining "what happened there" in the haunted site that we are going to "excavate" and explore.

In the research phase, we study how we become people. We learn how we become culturally and socially intelligible. We learn the conditions of past social existence. Through our research efforts, we establish a baseline for "what remains" from past occupations.

What is this performance relational field of entanglement, and how does it come into "play" in a "ghost excavation"? This is the subject of the next essay.

Photo 6: The "Ghost Excavation"

E. "Excavation" as Site-Specific Theatre

"Excavation has a unique role to play as a theatre where people may be able to produce their own pasts, pasts which are meaningful to them, not as expressions of a mythical heritage....Excavations need to become much more so than they are today....This is to advocate a socially engaged rather than a scientifically detached practice of excavation".

- **(Tilley, *Theatre as Archaeology*, 1989)**

An "excavation" of haunted space is essential for ghost research. This, however, is much more than "ghost hunt" entertainment. It is also different than a tech-based measurement of space. It is even more than a traditional archaeological excavation of physicality ("digging down") and site-defining parameters.

A "ghost excavation" is an entanglement with the past, not an entanglement with those present who come to excavate, explore, or attempt to engage that past. It can be (but is not) a place that allows other forms of contemporary production (such as historical re-enactment; ghost tour/investigation). If this occurs, that "other" contemporary production would not be relative to what occurred in the past. It would not entangle with what remains of that past in the present.

A haunted site is a **"contact zone" (cf. Pratt 2008)** that affords and enables various contextual encounters, an opportunity to be in contact with what remains embedded from perhaps multiple pasts. An entanglement relies on performance. This is discussed in this book as a relational archaeological approach.

Investigative performance, as **"theatre/archaeology (Pearson and Shanks 2001),** is nothing special or innovative when staged at an archaeological site. There is a long tradition of performance events at archaeological sites (cf. Hamilakis 2007). But what about an archaeological site (as ruin) and one that is perceived to be "haunted"? This is a largely unexplored venue. It is at these sites that we enact a performance "ghost excavation".

The "ghost excavation" is a form of site-specific theatre, something well-suited for a haunted location. Here is how Pavis (1998) defines site-specific theatre:

"The term refers to a staging and performance conceived on the basis of a place in the real world....a large part of the work has to do with researching a place, of an usual one that is imbued with history or permeated with atmosphere...." (1998:337).

A haunted site is, indeed, one that is "imbued with history" and "permeated with atmosphere".

Pearson and Shanks (2001), in speaking about a relation between theatre and archaeology, refer to **"the host and the ghost".** They consider the place is the "host", and the props and other performance elements are the "ghosts" that haunt that place (Kaye 2000:53).

In a "ghost excavation", we make no such distinction. What we bring to an "excavation" ("triggers" in the form of costuming, historical narratives, music, etc.), during our performance practices, do not "haunt" the place. We resonate (relate) to the past, so as to become entangled with it. We seek to "unearth" what remains (the "ghosts"). We don't intend adding to the "haunting" by including something not already performed there in the past. The space of our own work (the "excavation") is the same space as the performances that were enacted in the past (perhaps multiple pasts).

There is no "stage" or additional "props". We use, as much as possible, the environmental setting as it was used in the ethno-historical past where we are conducting our "excavations". We don't incorporate "tech overload" to document our performances. We used what "they" in the past used (for the most part). For example, we use lanterns or candles, not flashlights. This is about presence and (past) identity. It is about storytelling, through the execution of past (not contemporary) practices and behaviors.

The sense of place as being, or rather becoming, haunted has to be re-activated through performance, not waiting (and hoping) for something to happen. The "ghosts" need to be recalled through performances that entangle them. That act of relevance and relativity becomes a collective and shared experience of sociability.

That is the essence of a "ghost excavation" performance. A haunting is produced (re-produced) through sensorial practices ("triggers"), the performance scenarios, and the "afterlife" memory of the "ghost". This abandonment of linear time, and tech display/usage, creates an open ground, without artificial (or superficial) barriers. This permits various ontological possibilities to emerge.

Example: The Weyburn Project as Site-Specific Performance

The Weyburn Project was a site-specific performance using the Weyburn Mental Hospital in Weyburn,

Saskatchewan, Canada, as its location for an "excavation". The project **"used a complex overlay of narratives and experiences by combining memory, myth, and dream embedded in the 'host' building. Here the building itself draws focus and provides an archaeological or forensic site of investigation"**.

The performance at the site involved:

"a multi-layered exploration….an act of walking, looking, and excavating – a stripping away of layers to reveal the interpretation of space, place, culture, and history….(including) **legends that surround the building"**.

The performances were enacted around a series of "excavations", stories about the hospital, such that **"the building provides the history, legends, dreams, the ghosts that will make up the eventual performance"**. These myths, folklore, and legends, though many were unverifiable, were considered important **"artifacts"** of the archaeology of Weyburn.

The performances there took place in late August and early September of 2002, and allowed the audience **"to move through the real spaces of the past: to see, hear, smell, and touch….the sounds and silences of the building itself"**.

The Haunted Site

A. <u>Communication at a Haunted Site and in a Haunting Situation</u>

How do we interact with the past in haunted space, once fieldwork is undertaken there? How might contact, and communication with an interactive presence, be enabled? One approach might follow Roman Jakobson's ideas on communication. Though his structural analysis of language is no longer valid, his ideas on communication are still used today (cf. Bradford 2013).

According to Jakobson (1981), every verbal act consists of six elements. These are:

1. The addresser (the investigator);
2. The sent message (a "s.c.a.r." scenario);
3. The addressee (a "targeted" past presence);
4. The context ("excavating" a past layer of memory);
5. The same code (situational resonance that entangles past and present acts); and
6. The contact (a cultural "trigger" mechanism).

Communication is potentially achieved through an entanglement between what remains (past) and the communicative performance (present). The prerequisite for this communication is directed intentionality.

And this, as communication, is not about sharing messages (such as "you are dead"), or educating the other side ("This is" (referring to an audio recorder or tech device)). It is about starting and sustaining a social relation, the entanglement of contact, communication, and interaction. The less the entity is told about what came after their death, the better it is for communication to occur. This is because the social interaction is less traumatic.

B. Historical Re-Enactment: "The Emperor's New Clothes"

Many in ghost research give some importance to re-enactment as a stimulus for "awakening" haunting manifestations. But is it really a stimulus? If not, why not? The last three decades have witnessed the evolution of historical re-enactment transformed into a global social and cultural phenomenon (Agnew 2004; 2007). Has this increased the global reporting of anomalous or haunting phenomena into sites and spaces where these re-enactments occur?

Perhaps not. And this may be due to the lack of real social entanglements between the past and contemporary re-enactors regarding the use of knowledge about the past. A recent ethnographic study of historical re-enactment in Poland and Sweden (Kobialka 2013) suggests that **"it is not knowledge that was relevant in re-enactment, but things, objects that looked as if they were from the Viking Age" (2013: 144).** There is a similar logic with other historical re-enactments as well.

Is historical re-enactment a simulacra (Pawleta 2011:17), a "copy" that does not refer to any original historical narrative? Are historical re-enactments real scenarios that produce social relations with past presence? Does re-enacting transform a re-enactor back into an entanglement that produces an emerging haunting presence?

It is the "bounded" rules that govern historical re-enactment, not another reality. These rules ensure that "authenticity" is maintained within the event. But this is a rule of historicity, not ethnography. To be historically accurate is not the same as ethnographic immersion. This is because, in the latter, once a relationship is established, it continues through the entanglement until communication with an emerging presence ceases.

In an historical re-enactment, the past does not emerge and acted upon by the re-enactor. Without participation, no entanglement with the past occurs. A "ghost excavation" <u>directly</u> relates to what is left of the past. A re-enactment relates to a "live" contemporary audience: fellow re-enactors and the observing public.

An historical re-enactment attempts to mirror the past: to be historical. A "ghost excavation" attempts to "unearth" a particular situational past: to be ethnographic – perform/observe/participate. During an historical re-enactment, there is no time travel involved (present to past; past to present), notwithstanding the "wargasm" sensed by some re-enactors.

This is because a "haunting" and the "ghosts" are not observed. No social relationship is established. A re-enactment begins and ends with a pre-ordained program for contemporary public consumption, not one "targeting" a particular past audience. Historical re-enactment is a fascination with mirroring the historical past. It is not concerned with "unearthing" the "what" or "who" that may remain from the past.

Photo 7: An Historical Re-Enactment

C. The Use of "Relational Archaeologies" at Haunted Locations

Can relational linkages be formed as social transactions between humans and "ghosts"? Can these transactions emerge, and become present, across space and through time? Are there contextual paths that entangle beings? Can we attain an ontological status for once-living human entities through the tracing of material or sensory signatures as they affect or are being affected by 21st c. investigators who are attuned to the entanglements that existed in the past?

I propose that the answer to these questions is all in the affirmative. There is a way to "unbound" entities and create **"meshworks" (Ingold 2011)**, an entwined field of relations that can become manifest as part of contemporary reality. This can be achieved by an intentional flow and movement of people, "things", and "other" entities that create an entanglement between a past and the present.

With this entanglement, I propose, a wall is torn down. We are no longer contained in a reality populated by knowing and knowable subjects (living humans) and entities to be (perhaps) known at some time in the future. Instead, we have worlds filled with living beings, defined by the emergence of particular social relations and entanglements.

This reality cannot be separated into binary oppositions (human/ghost; normal/paranormal; past/present; presence/absence). It cannot be enclosed within analytical parameters (science vs. "fringe") because to understand one, in this entanglement, requires an acceptance and appreciation of the role and position within an expanding field populated by "others".

A "ghost excavation" is performance-observed. If something becomes of that performance, a participation in that interaction follows. In a "ghost excavation", the team both experiences and observes this performance and any intentional communication that comes from it. As co-participants in a past ethnographic encounter, a "ghost excavation" is an inter-subjective methodology.

This is producing knowledge through experience, not measurement. It alters our state of being with that "other" reality. This is acquiring knowledge through relating to a process of entanglement. There is empathy, as a desire to be in a real human relationship with the "ghost", not one of power through commands and demands.

A "ghost excavation" is thus fieldwork that is an embodied experience of relatedness. A haunting emerges in our moments of relating, through the performance practices. This process of "relating" and entanglement has a deep history in social interactions between the living and the dead, and features of the landscape, such as in Andean South America (see Viveiros de Castro 1998).

This approach is a socio-centric, rather than egocentric view of interaction and communication, one that should be applied, I propose, to haunted space. The investigator, in this view, serves as a social being in a node of an open network connecting other beings, spaces, and things.

The modern view of a person as a **"coherent, bounded, individualized, intentional, the locus of thought, action, and belief, the beneficiary of a unique biography" (Rose 1998:3)** persona may be in error. This "persona" may not be transferable in haunted space, where multiple (and perhaps different) ethnographic cultures may still linger.

Here, a typical "ghost hunt", where "anything goes", and where people feel they can do what they see on TV (a bounded system) may be highly inappropriate. This "coherent" and bounded individualism is certainly not characteristic of many contemporary world cultures, and **"might be wholly inappropriate for ethnographic and archaeological studies of other cultures" (Hutson 2010:3).**

"Who" may manifest at a haunted site is, in some instances, a "bounded ghost", acting without contemporary reason or intention. Consideration must be given for the possibility and acknowledgement of past social class, gender differences, ethnicity, and other aspects of identity not fully taken into account in a typical "ghost hunt" or "paranormal investigation".

In a "ghost excavation", we aim to create a relation of "subjectification", as a process of becoming:

"The process by which humans become intelligible people accepted members of a society" (Hutson 2010:6).

We do this through performance, the enactment of particular contextual scenarios in specific spaces that serve as "cues" in identifying us (the "excavation team") as one of "them" (a member of a particular past culture and social group that remain "attached" to a particular site).

In this relational model, binary barriers are erased (life/death; normal/paranormal). This opens up the subject (a haunting), allowing the outside world (the present) to penetrate it and re-constitute it. Interaction in haunted space – the performance practices that leave recordable traces- can now be understood to be <u>related</u> to the production and re-production (as in a haunting) of a fragment of past social life. This is identity formation, both contemporary and past, becoming present and entangled.

In a "ghost excavation", what manifests is never totally foreign or paranormal. This is because we have established a context through our performance practices. We know, through ethno-historical research, "what happened there", "who" was there, and what and "whom" may be unearthed through our "digging" into particular roles and situations. We have a working knowledge of the layers of memory and the matrix associations through which we "dig".

This background data, supplemented by a peripatetic daytime "walk-thru", does not remain in the background during fieldwork. It directs us, gives us "clues", and it focuses us to what is in the foreground. It might not provide us with a complete or final understanding, but it does provide us with a baseline for further excavations.

This helps us dissolve the boundaries between subject and object, past and present, and absence and presence. This is because that past presence was already there. In a "ghost excavation", it merely becomes present during the fieldwork. Those traces and fragments of what remains are present today, and we are not experientially separated from the past. We can "unearth" the effects of past activity that remain around us (in haunted space), as at traditional archaeological sites (cf. Fowler 2013).

We recover these traces and fragments of a continuing past through relational archaeologies. This is a matter of both epistemology (how we obtain an understanding of contemporary reality = P.O.P.) and ontology (what may remain). A "ghost excavation" describes and transforms reality by re-covering what really is there from material and sensory remains that are normally absent ("unexcavated").

Entities of various kinds (residual elements and interactive apparitional) are contemporary past assemblages of entanglements that become present due to relational social interactions of other entities (the "excavation team"), materials ("targeting cues"), and behaviors (contextual performances. They all serve as "actants" (Latour 1993) that affect contemporary reality.

This puts social relationships (an entangled cultural resonance and identity) first, as opposed to measurements and "demands and commands". It is thinking how and understanding why a haunting emerges (is "unearthed") and becomes present from this identity and that relationship.

Also, this assumes that a haunting is a social history (not a para-history), and that past relationships (and the memory of that experience) shape a haunting (and what materializes). This social entanglement has an effect on what, when, and who manifests during a "ghost excavation". Thus, I propose, any traces and fragments that emerge from a "ghost excavation" are haunting legacies of past entanglements, and their manifestation in contemporary space is relative to that identity and social relativity that is made during performance practices in a "ghost excavation".

The meaning of a haunting that becomes present, therefore, becomes entirely dependent upon the performance context. It is this identifiable social context, relative to contemporary performances, that makes this connective relationship possible.

It is not the instrument sweep that defines it. It is not a general "demand and command" that causes its appearance. It is not a simple question (such as "Is anyone here?") that provides an answer. In ghost research, we should be studying past practices and situations, and what remains of this. This is not a "ghost" or a "paranormal" event!

A haunted location is an expansive field (more so with the addition of contemporary layers through "ghost hunting"). It cannot be confined to borders and "boxed" into a neat package called "paranormal". This is because there remain countless haunting legacies left by the entanglements of social interactions that involved past realities.

We must focus our efforts, not on advancing technologies, but on how these relational social relationships arose, persist, and manifest today based on their material and sensory legacies of what and who still remains from these relationships.

If "evidence" is a specific entanglement between performance, manifestation, theory of cultural resonance ("relational archaeologies") and recording equipment (such as RT-EVP audio recorder, video, and photographic triangulation), in each act of participatory inquiry, then a "ghost excavation" is building a solid baseline for evidential data.

And through a "follow-up" (participating in a manifesting situation), it extends (and builds) the traces of this social relation with past presence from one scenario configuration to the next. It is making more connections in a web of relational (entangled) associations.

In summary, the concepts of emergence (a "haunting"), lines of becoming present (performance practices) create (or re-store) an assemblage of experiences and memories that manifest in haunted space. A haunting (and its perception) does not rely on identifying a baseline context against which the elements of the phenomenon must be measured (such as EMF "spikes"; temperature fluctuations, etc.), typical in "ghost hunting" lore.

There should be no presumption of a single set of organizing rules which must be put into effect, or to have an effect, for a haunting to occur, or be verified as such ("the place is haunted because...."). What is important to the emergence of a haunting, I propose, is the primacy of past and contemporary social relationships that are directly relative to what occurred in a space at a given time in history. That relation must form an entanglement between what occurred there, and what performances are enacted there today.

Figure 2: The Entanglement"

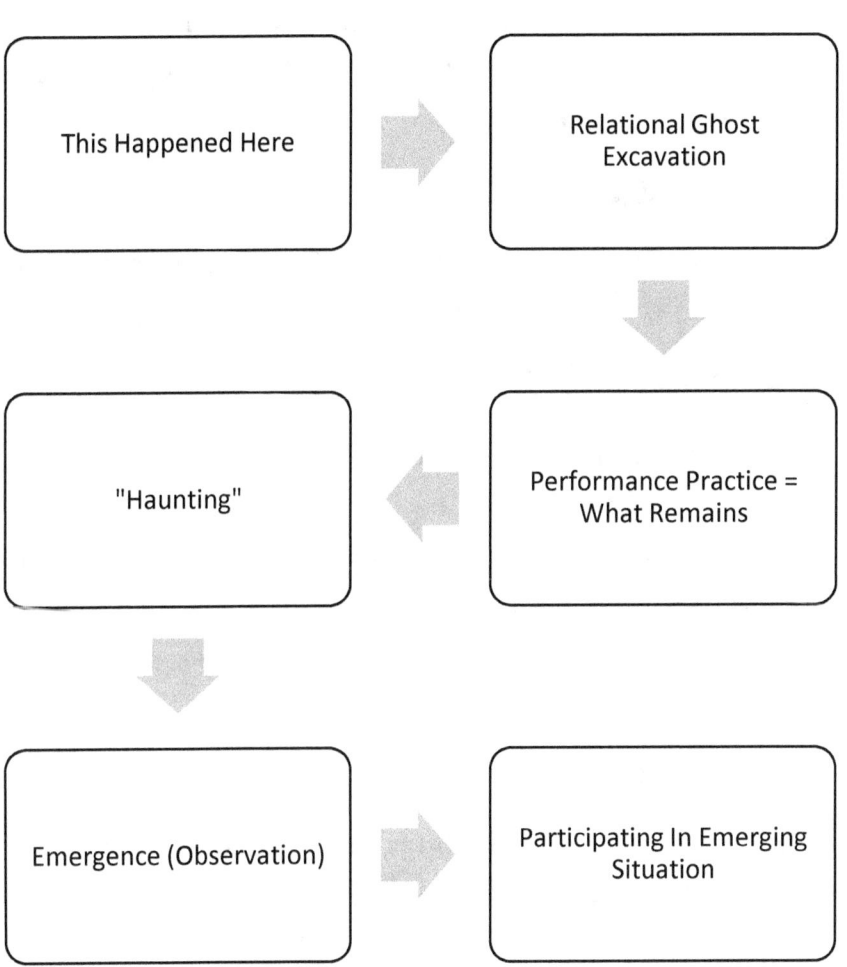

D. The Negativity of Non-Relational "Ghost Hunting"

"Anything – caught at a particular place and moment – enfolds within its constitution the history of relations that have brought it there".

- Ingold (2011:160)

"Anything that has a causal effect or potential is defined as ontologically real".

- Wallace (2011:7).

"We are ourselves producers of archaeological materials. We do little more than add a new archaeological episode to the existence of places and things that have often already known a long series of functions and uses….We add new strata of information…."

- Olivier (2001:180).

We are all entangled within the fieldwork we do, be it "ghost hunting", "paranormal investigation", or a "ghost excavation". The characteristics of that entanglement do affect what we study and the results of that study.

If there is no relation (social or cultural) to past special occupations, there is a weak entanglement (or none at all). That weak (or lack of) entanglement produces an accretion (additional) elements embedded onto the space and site. At the same time, it suppresses or even erases prior networks of entanglement. A "ghost hunt" or "paranormal investigation" in historical haunted space, without using relational elements of past entanglements (such as advanced technologies; different dress codes; non-contextual behaviors; and different speech patterns/vocabularies), can produce these accretions. They add additional contemporary layers. They do not help to document the emergence of historical past presences. They create a "contemporary haunting"!

A "ghost hunt" or a "paranormal investigation", without resonating social entanglements, instead of isolating and defining historically-emerging phenomenon, extend the phenomena that becomes present to include contemporary manifestations (in the future). A final resolution to whether a site is haunted by past presence cannot be reached due to this new entanglement of added technology and behaviors.

This creates a situation that is "paranormal" because the old remains out of reach due to this new entanglement! As a result of similar repetitions of these entanglements (re: "ghost tourism"), the present and the future suppress the historical past. The "haunting" is re-configured and enfolds as a contemporary haunting phenomenon. Fowler (2013) states as much, when he says that relationality **"also exhibits the traces, residues, or legacies of past interactions" (2013:63).**

Photo 8: Is this a Proper Entanglement with the Past?

Performance

A. <u>Do We Measure or Perform?</u>

The problem with measuring space is the concept of translation:

- What does elevated EMF really mean (in the context of a cultural haunting)?
- What does temperature variation mean? Is there a difference, important in determining particular haunting phenomena, between a rise and a fall in temperature?
- What does a deviation from a baseline represent? What is the basis for the baseline?

What are "ghost hunters" and "paranormal investigators" really measuring? Is it the present? Is it the past? Is it the past in the present? Is it a residual of a past atmospheric condition, or is a present, past moment? What really does the measurement mean?

Measured space is a mediation, not a <u>direct</u> connect to (or a relation with) a past presence, or to what remains from a particular past entanglement of space. A translation suggests a degree of misunderstanding, if one does not fully understand how a space was produced in the past! Measurement is a "hunt" for meaning. Measurements establish discontinuities. Is this "discontinuity" a "haunting"? This is NOT what remains. It establishes a difference. It maintains the boundary. It justifies the binary (past/present; presence/absence, etc.)!

A measurement divides space. Having divided it, we encounter traces and fragments that further disconnect us from an entanglement with the past. In order to understand, we try to connect the pieces through measured translations. Where is the sociability in this lack of performance?

In a "ghost excavation", we move in the opposite direction. We attempt to recover continuity: what remains after the event of production. What are the "signs" of this continuity? This requires research into how a particular space was produced.

We create hypotheses as storyboards: resonating acts that relate directly, through performance practices, with what occurred in the past as social entanglements. There is no mediation. It is a direct communication to determine the type of presence that still remains. It is a series of investigative performance acts, hits and misses. This is not a "hunt". It is an "excavation" of past social entanglements!

B. Performance: Altering the Apparitional State of Being

"….Homo performans….one set of human beings may come to know themselves better through observing and/or participating in performances generated and presented by another set of human beings".

- **Victor Turner, Anthropologist**

Through performance, an entanglement with the past is initiated, as one set of entities (investigators) comes to know better, and become socially involved, with another group of beings (the "ghosts" that haunt the present).

In a "ghost excavation", a performance is purposeful enactment, not re-enactment. We perform in haunted space to a potential audience that becomes present, sometimes to one that was never there. This is an "excavation". We don't know what remains remain at a site, until we "dig" it out through performance, as we become entangled with what remains.

The purpose of these performance practices is to alter the cognitive state of the participants (the investigators). This is not a form of re-enactor "wargasm". It is to change a near automatic engagement of "ghost hunting" practices (such as scan, measure, monitor, demand and command) to something more relational to what occurred in the past. The "zombie-like" display on "hunts" comes close, in most instances, to something completely purposeless.

A "ghost hunt" is not investigative performance. And there is little social reason for a "ghost" to emerge if the possibility of affecting a reason is not present. In order to be affective and relational, a performance must induce an altered state (as well) in the apparition. They must become engaged with the investigative performance, entangled in the experience. This results in a willingness to communicate.

Performance is an accomplishment. It is not a measurement. It involves taking social action, not recording a change in ambient temperature or in EMF levels. It certainly doesn't ask them (the "ghosts") to perform to the instruments!

In a "ghost excavation", there is reinforced feedback. It is not a stimulus-response system. It is a performance loop, an entanglement that results in a social relationship. If the "ghost" responds, the social entanglement expands. In some cases, it is the "ghost" that will initiate a participatory request, rather than the investigator. This is what occurred during our "ghost excavations" at Burnside Bridge on the Antietam battlefield in Maryland (see Sabol 2013).

Past performance is emergent, and participation is important after a manifestation occurs. This involves investigative "attention" to what just occurred. This immediate attention and directed (and contextual) response is usually lacking in a "ghost hunt", where a manifestation is not usually immediately detected, and immediately participated in by the investigators.

Research ensures performance compatibility (scenarios that are contextual, resonating, and relational). Otherwise, as in a "ghost hunt", a tech "performance, tied to demand and command (or a space that is merely "monitored", not performed in) results in unpredictable manifestations and cultural behaviors.

Performance "flow" (relationality) is critical. This is to make the performance acts appear effortless, sincere, and natural. This is why we use trained actors in our "ghost excavations". That is why the investigator, as actor, is not directly involved in the observation of what is emerging.

The investigative "performers" remain in character, while a team of investigative-observers controls the recording process. The observers also give "cues" to the investigator-performer when something (or someone) emerges. This allows the performance to become a part of the emergence, without affecting the "flow" of the excavation process. This "flow" is called "P.O.P." (Perform-Observe-Participate).

Photo 9: The "P.O.P." Process in Action

C. Performance and the "Afterlife Mind"

In any location (a physical structure or landscape), individual and group social and habitual performance practices, operating in unison with particular cultural codes, were performed. At a haunted location, some of these past behavioral practices continue. It is up to the investigative team to "crack the (cultural) code" of what remains of these past practices that may be embedded in particular spaces.

A haunted space is experiential space, retaining fragments and traces of memory, experience, and emotion, not measured readings. Couclelis (1992) offers a view of this space:

"Experiential space....is the space human beings actually experience before it is passed through the filters of scientific analysis...."(1992:229).

In haunted space, one must follow particular codes of cultural engagement to become part of a past entanglement. This differs as to time period and culture. A relational performance does something. It can make things happen. Judith Butler (1993) suggests that performance can **"reproduce effects through reiteration" (1993:20).** This is repeating acts that were done in the past, entangling two worlds into one: the present and the past.

The memory of these repetitive behaviors and dialogues of social action become inscribed at haunted locations. Memory is an active process, and this inscription will form part of the **"sedimentation"** (layered strata) of social memory at haunted locations (see Connerton 1989). Is there still an "active" being behind what goes on at haunted locations, or is it just a "mindless" residual, a memory without intent or purpose?

George H. Mead (1934) proposed the notion that "mind" arises in social interaction. For Mead, there is no mind within an interactive social environment, If we think of the "mind" as external to the body, and the brain internal, then what survives after the death of the physical body is an "afterlife mind", since the "mind" is not dependent on the body (following Mead).

It is proposed that an active apparitional haunting can become present, as this "afterlife mind", when it is entangled within a relational social environment, such as we initiate and perform in a "ghost excavation".

If, in death, this "afterlife mind" still has memories (and remembers), then a social relation can exist with another (such as the contemporary investigator), if and when the "ghost" recognizes a similar mental state with this "other" (the investigator).

If the contemporary investigator is acting in a way that an "afterlife mind" recognizes, an entangled connection can possibly occur. Thus, a contemporary performance could allow one to "unearth" what remains of "afterlife minds" at haunted sites.

The linkage of past entanglements to ongoing experience (past memory and contemporary investigative performance) is essential, I propose, for a underlined controlled manifestation to occur in haunted space. The haunted space becomes, not a "paranormal" zone or a space of terror, but rather a safe "practice" area. It becomes a space of sociability.

In this space of sociability, based on relational elements between the "past" and the present, there occurs a transformation. Time unfolds. A haunting emerges. And a relational performance is the behavioral tool that allows us, in the present, to present ourselves (contextually) to "others". Contemporary performances achieve a manifesting presence because of this entanglement to a particular past layer of memory from an embedded "afterlife mind".

In a "ghost excavation", we willingly engage with a particular past presence (or "afterlife mind"), by knowing "who" occupied a specific space and place through prior research. We enter that contemporary (haunted) space in an altered state, one different from the present. Though performance is framed to be relational, we don't raise our expectations of success. Those who remain can (and sometimes do) break this social frame and not communicate, if they are not "satisfied" with the performance (or were non-conformist in life).

I propose that these social performances are necessary for human sociability (even with "afterlife minds"), and that "other" performances are what survive physical death. They are what haunt us today. I further suggest that a contemporary relational performance can lead to transformations in space, resulting in a past social entanglement becoming present today.

Anthropologist Victor Turner once stated that performance allows us the freedom to alter the normal structures of social life, entering into alternative other structures. One such alternative (though not "paranormal") structure is a "haunting". It is an alternative state where two or more entities (one past and one contemporary) connect to each other in a social relational way. These social entanglements are twice-behaved behaviors (Schechner 1990:43):

- They were performed in the past as "natural" social behaviors; and
- They are re-performed in the present as a haunting becoming present.

D. Latourian Actants and the Emergence of a Haunting

A haunted location is a place where one might perceive and experience a sensual, interactive, albeit different, world. At a haunted site, this can involve the entanglement of multiple (and varying) layers of embedded memory. Each of these layers may form the grounds for relational "excavating" archaeologies. That is why we must "target" our excavation practices to each possible layer of memory or "S.C.A.R." that may remain embedded in particular spaces at the haunted location.

A "ghost excavation" rests its "excavating" practices on understanding commonalities (or relations) of experience and social interaction. These represent particular intra-cultural past entanglements, and trans-temporal entangled possibilities in the future (present). An "excavation" proposes that **"the very physicality of the body (as a performance "tool") imposes a schema on space through which it** (the entanglement) **may be experienced and understood" (Tilley 1994:16).**

The work of Bruno Latour offers a model of interaction (as a form of entanglement) as a network of **"actants"**. An "actant" is anything (ideas and beliefs are also "actants") that has an effect on something else. In a "ghost excavation", the investigator, as performer, is an "actant", as well as the "triggers" he/she uses (such as clothing and speech patterns). The "triggers" serve as memory "cues". They are also a form of "object animation", since they are meant to "animate" action in haunted space.

The contextual scenarios that are performed at a haunted location in a particular space are an "assemblage" of "actants" whose purpose is to create an entanglement with the past. For Latour, it is this "assemblage" that acts, and "actants" (as "triggers") articulate particular assemblages (scenarios) through specific "propositions".

A "proposition" is **"an occasion given to different entities to enter into contact" (Latour 1999:141).** For example, on a haunted Civil War battlefield during a "ghost excavation", one "proposition" would be the enactment of a "roll-call" (a role within the "culture of war"). The "actants" would involve an investigator (as military officer), and "triggers" (use of bugle call to muster the men; names of a particular company of soldiers who fought and died on that battlefield).

This "proposition" would be enacted in a particular battlefield space ("K.O.C.O.A.") where this act and role would have been enacted during the Civil War (such as an identified "cover and concealed area", and enacted before movement to an "avenue of approach" toward the military objective).

The use of "actants", "assemblages", and "propositions" is a form of relational archaeological methodology meant to establish a socially-relevant entanglement in a particular haunted space:

Figure 3: Relational Methodology

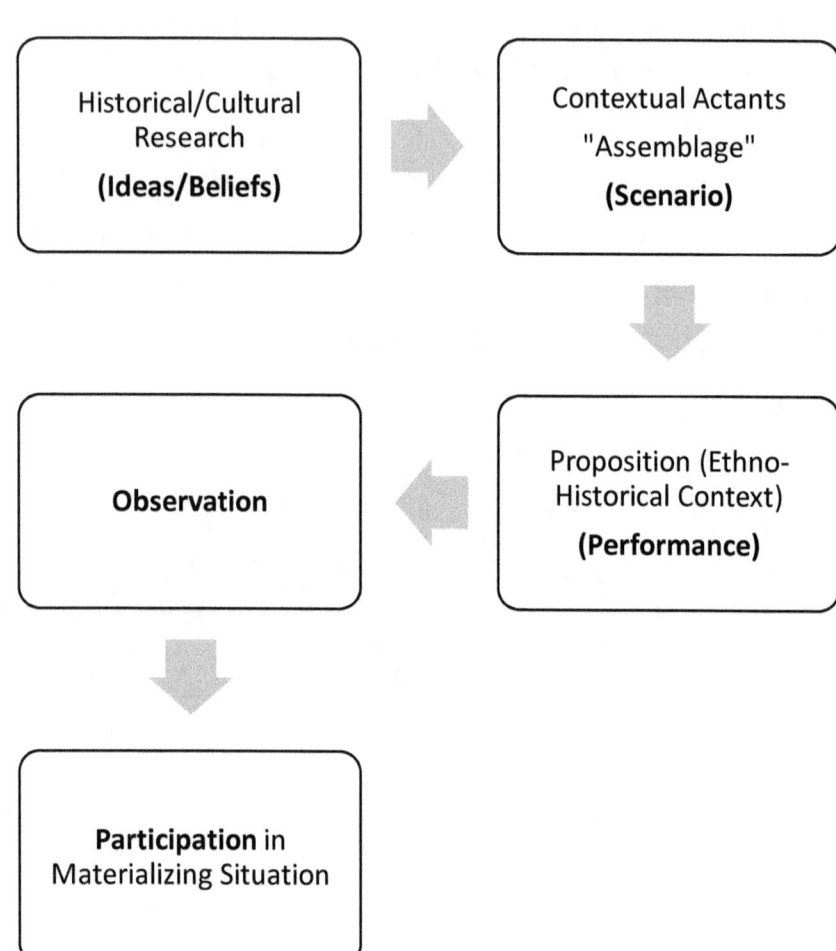

If the "actants", "assemblage", and "proposition" are strongly relative (and resonate), and there is "active" past presence, it may produce a haunting manifestation.

The clear message of this "excavation" methodology is to establish a baseline for a social relationship (entanglement) to become present in a potential haunting, allowing it to emerge through resonance (similar entanglement as in the past) and recognition (the memory of it by an "afterlife mind"). This relational methodology is based on the concept that "things" (sensory elements), places (spaces), and entities all have "lives", affects, and effects of their own in haunted space, and in contemporary reality.

A weak or non(mis)-use of a relational "assemblage" can produce a contemporary haunting which adds to the palimpsest of layers in haunted space. It also could erase previous past layers and/or suppress them. A suppression of past haunting layers requires a "deeper excavation" in order to "unearth" them through a "stronger" contextual assemblage of a socially-producing entanglement.

Photo 10: The "Jogger" at Burnside Bridge (Non-Contextual Actant)

Latour (1999) frames each entity he wishes to study as both "actant" and "reference". A "reference" is something (someone) that circulates in a chain of interactions with other "actants" and becomes identified as such and transformed in the process.

This concept of "reference" is incorporated into the "P.O.P." method in a "ghost excavation":

- Perform assemblage;
- Observe any emergence; and
- Participate with "what" and "who" emerges.

We build relationships and entanglements through "P.O.P.", extending our identity interaction, and entanglement into other "assemblages" relative to "what" and "who" just emerged. Subsequent "assemblages" are based on what emerged in a previously-performed "assemblage. We continue to participate to ever expand the process of relational social interaction/entanglement until communication with the entity (or entities) discontinues.

At Burnside Bridge, on the Antietam battlefield in Maryland, what emerged from our "roll-call" assemblage was the manifestation of particular past presences. These were particular soldiers of the 11th Connecticut ("Dayton" and "Flint"), both of whom died during the 1st assault toward Burnside Bridge on September 17, 1862.

Having established a possible entanglement with them, we continued to participate with them in other enacted assemblages (recreating their charge toward the bridge along the Rohrbach farm road). This resulted in the recording of men fighting along this road (see www.ghostexcavation.com to listen to these recordings).

Fowler (2013) states that assemblages may endure from one relationship to another **"if some of the relationship previously articulating those features persist" (2013:63).** The emergence of "Dayton" and "Flint", in "assemblages" (as a repeated entanglement of "actants") in the production of field data, becomes a "circulating reference" where **"the word reference designates the quality of the chain in its entirety" (Latour 1999:69).**

The initial "assemblage" (the "roll-call" scenario), by continuing its entanglement to subsequent "assemblages", reinforces its potential as an investigative tool that may "unearth" still other emerging presences at a haunted location. It does suggest that that a "reference" may exist since we encountered it (through the continued manifestations of both "Dayton" and "Flint") in a subsequent recorded (and contextual) "assemblage".

We can strengthen that "reference" by continuing, in subsequent "excavations", to enact "relational" assemblages through chains of relations (Inherent Military Probability or I.M.P. of the "culture of war" of the American Civil War in particular military "K.O.C.O.A." spaces) embedded in previous assemblages.

In a "ghost excavation", as "materializations" emerge through performed "assemblages", we can say that an analysis of this data involves the simultaneous (as recorded via our RT-EVP devices) entanglement of the following elements:

- "Manifesting" sensory elements of this "culture of war";
- Co-equal with the use of contextual "actants", "assemblages", and "propositions"; and our
- "live" experience of what emerged (became present).

It is this "network" of entanglement that acts as a whole, and comes together as we "P.O.P." it!

The emergence of "past presence" in this network is an "affect" in a "ghost excavation". This "affect" is any means in which that emergence can "affect" other entities, both past and present. The potential of these "affects" depends upon the network ("actants"; "assemblage", and "proposition").

Thus, the contemporary investigator plays a vital role in entering those entanglements that manifest from the past and remain to haunt the present. Our social interactions, in a "ghost excavation", with the traces and residuals of past entanglements are critical in the emergence of haunting phenomenon.

What and "who" remain can emerge from the entangled process of creating relational and contextual social bonds and actions ("actants", "assemblages", and "propositions") during the "excavation" itself. We need to work with, go through, and over the boundaries set by the popular trope of "ghost hunting" and "paranormal investigation". There is not a single world out there, bounded by physical geography, scientific materialism, or contemporary reality.

We cannot make mistakes that hinder our "leap" beyond the "paranormal". As Fowler (2013) says, in reference to"**relational realist archaeology**", can be applied to ghost research:

"**We should not try to separate statements into 'facts' and things that are not 'facts', this does not descend into an 'anything goes' relativism in which any translation is as good as any other**" (2013:60).

We cannot, for sake of unity, parity, and "political correctness" let anyone do what they want in an investigation of haunted space, simply because "nothing has been proven". That "free to do all" creates further barriers by building "paranormal walls" (and creating new "live" haunting images for future investigators).

Alberti and Bray (2009) have argued that we need to understand that past entanglements relate to both differing beliefs and ways (acts) of being. We must not impose contemporary entanglements (tech-based; "demand and command") onto those from the past, and expect that a measured "reading" is a response from a past presence.

Knowledge about (and understanding of) a haunting is not about a single (or even multiple) "deviant" measurements. It must include the whole "assemblage": all the "manifestations" within the "assemblages" and propositions". This understanding involves a change to social reality, not something just measured. It involves all the entities that remain, not just one past event. And each may require a <u>different</u> social entanglement.

This is re-working the site, arriving at new possibilities through these social entanglements. We have seen this entanglement evolve and expand at Burnside Bridge. Each subsequent "excavation" increased the strength of our relational entanglement with those who remain. At Burnside Bridge, the past is emerging continually (see Sabol 2013) for more details on the Burnside Bridge "ghost excavations").

In archaeology,

"the material identities ascribed to things are not their essential properties but the result of relationships of people and things...." (Holtorf 2008:166).

The same can be said, I propose, during an investigation of haunted space. What "manifests" (is "unearthed") is not assigned as something "paranormal" based on its lack of "current" explanation or its deviant measured ambiance. In a "ghost excavation", a "manifestation" is assigned agency because of its social entanglement both to the "propositions" we enact <u>and</u> its relational association(s) to what occurred in that particular space in the past.

An archaeological excavation alters a site, leaving <u>contemporary</u> "scars". As Michael Shanks (2012) states:

"....in order to know the past, we dig, we intervene and destroy" (2012:91).

He also says that **"in order to preserve the past, it must be creatively reused...." (Ibid: 91).** A "ghost excavation" does this by unearthing what remains of <u>past</u> "s.c.a.r.s." through relational archaeologies as a social entanglement with the past. A "ghost excavation" uses contextual, not intrusive, field performance practices.

<u>Note:</u>

Not all relational "propositions" (contextual scenarios) are effective, or <u>equally</u> effective. We must strive to develop "propositions" that are well-related to those from the past, and are effective in engaging particular past presences. They must be sufficiently articulated (and executed) to form effective "assemblages" (relational "propositions", associated "actants", and non-intrusive recording devices).

Summary

Currently, there is no way to prove that a haunting is occurring, or that ghostly presence exists at a location that is said to be haunted. But we can build a case for it through social entanglements and relational archaeologies. In the immiscible time of haunted space, or one potentially haunted, there is no time frame. There is only "now", and what happened in this space or place.

These entanglements with space and place remain, as fragments and traces of memory fields. In haunted space, there is no "before", something that occurred previously, if it still is occurring "now".

If one endlessly investigates locations, some groups even do this two or three different times (and locations) in a single weekend, asking the same questions, and using the same methods (scan, demand/command, measure, and monitor) for months (even years), then one is stuck in a "haunting time". "You" are the "ghost", not the "ghost hunter" or "paranormal investigator!

What have "you" learned from all these investigations? Nothing! "You" are a "residual", in an endless recorded loop! What are you "hunting" for – that "Holy Grail"? Are you using the "hunt" as a personal "drug", the same "fix" that needs to be satisfied often?

Isn't it about time to alter your state of mind, and how you do ghost research and paranormal investigations at perceived haunted locations? It is difficult and a challenge to change:

"When we are faced with information that contradicts beliefs (and practices) **we hold, we tend to reject the information or interpret it in a way that allows us to keep our beliefs...." (Joseph Campbell).**

But to deny other possibilities, other ways of doing something, is to become that "ghost". Accept that altered state described here, and sense what can manifest! This altered state of consciousness occurs, in ghost research, when one departs from the popular trope of "ghost hunting", and from what is recognized as the everyday, contemporary cultural beliefs, expressions, and behaviors of a "ghost hunt culture".

Bibliography

Aarnio, K. 2007. *Superstitious, Magical, and Paranormal Beliefs: An Integrative Model. Journal of Research in Personality 41: 731-744.*

Agnew, V. 2004. *Introduction: What is Reenactment? Criticism* 46(7): 327-339.

2007. *History's Affective Turn: Historical Re-Enactment and its Work in the Present. Rethinking History* 11(3): 299-312.

Alberti, B. and T. Bray. 2009. *Introduction. Cambridge Archaeological Journal* 19(3): 337-343.

Barth, F. 1987. *Cosmologies in the Making: A Generative Approach to Cultural Variation in Inner New Guinea.* Cambridge: Cambridge University Press.

Barthes, Roland. 1977. *Image, Music, Text.* New York: Hill and Wang.

1987. *Criticism and Truth.* London: Athlone Press.

Bates, Brian. 1987. *The Way of the Actor: A Path to Knowledge and Power.* Boston: Shambhala Publications.

Boyd, Brian. 2002. *The Myth Makers: Archaeology in Doctor Who* in *Digging Holes in Popular Culture: Archaeology and Science Fiction.* M. Russell (Editor). Oxbow Books, pp. 30-37.

Bradford, R. 2013. *Roman Jakobson: Life, Language, and Poetics.* London.

Butler, Judith. 1993. *Performance Acts and Gender Constitution: An Essay in Phenomenology and Feminist Thought* in G.E. Case (Editor) *Performing Feminisms: Feminist Critical Theory and Theatre.* Baltimore: John Hopkins University Press, pp. 270-282.

Connerton, Paul. 1989. *How Societies Remember.* Cambridge: Cambridge University Press.

Conzen, Michael. 1994. *The Making of the American Landscape.* London: Routledge.

Couclelis, H. 1992. *Location, Place, Region, and Space* in R.F. Adler, M.G. Marcus, and J.M. Olson (Editors) *Geography's Inner Worlds: Pervasive Themes in Contemporary American Geography.* New Brunswick, New Jersey: Rutgers University Press, p. 215-233.

Cua Lin, Bliss. 2009. *Translating Time: Cinema, the Fantastic, and Temporal Critique.* Durham: Duke University Press.

Danet, B. 1997. *Books, Letters, Documents: The Changing Aesthetics of Texts in Late Print Culture.* *Journal of Material Culture* 2: 5-38.

Dejarlais, Robert. 1996. *Struggling Along* in *Things as They Are: New Directions in Phenomenological Anthropology.* Edited by Michael Jackson. Bloomington: Indiana University Press, pp. 70-93.

Eco, Umberto. 1990. *A Theory of Semiotics.* Bloomington: Indiana University Press.

Eiseley, Loren. 1972. *The Night Country.* New York: Charles Scribner's Sons.

1975. *All the Strange Hours: The Excavation of a Life.* New York: Charles Scribner's Sons.

Fowler, Chris. 2013. *The Emergent Past: A Relational Realist Archaeology of Early Bronze Age Mortuary Practices.* Oxford: Oxford University Press.

Geertz, Clifford. 1973. *The Interpretation of Cultures.* New York: Basic Books.

Hamilakis, Y. 2007. *The Nation and its Ruins: Antiquity, Archaeology, and National Imagination in Greece.* Oxford: Oxford University Press.

Heidegger, M. 1971. *Poetry, Language, Thought.* A. Hofsadter (Translation). New York: Harper & Row.

Holtorf, Cornelius. 2008. *Notes on the Life History of a Pot Sherd* in *Reading Archaeology: An Introduction.* Edited by Robert J. Muckle. Peterborough, Ontario, Canada: Broadview press, pp. 156-169.

Hutson, Scott R. 2010. *Dwelling, Identity, and the Maya: Relational Archaeology at Chunchucmil.* New York: Altamira Press.

Hymes, Dell. 1981. *In Vein I Tried to Tell You: Essays in Native American Ethnopoetics.* Philadelphia: University of Pennsylvania Press.

Ingold, Tim. 2000. *Perception of the Environment: Essays in Livelihood, the Dwelling, and Skill.* London: Routledge.

2011. *Being Alive: Essays on Movement, Knowledge, and Description.* London: Routledge.

Jakobson, R. 1981. *Linguistics and Poetics in Selected Writings, Vol. III: Poetry of Grammar and Grammar of Poetry.* The Hague.

Karlstrom, Anna. 2012. *Authenticity Through Performance: The Practice of a Concept Within Contemporary Southeast Asian Heritage Discourse.*

Paper presented at Inaugural Conference of the Association of Critical Heritage Studies 'Re/theorization of Heritage', Gothenburg, 5-8 June.

Kaye, Nick. 2000. *Site-Specific Art.* London: Routledge.

Kirk, Trevor. 2006. *Materiality, Personhood, and Monumentality in Early Neolithic Britain. Cambridge Archaeological Journal* 16(3): 333-347.

Kobialka, Dawid. 2013. *The Mask(s) and Transformers of Historical Re-Enactment: Material Culture and Contemporary Vikings. Current Swedish Archaeology* 21: 141-161.

Latour, Bruno. 1993. *We Have Never Been Modern.* Cambridge, Mass: Cambridge University Press.

1999. *Pandora's Hope: Essays on the Reality of Science Studies.* Cambridge, Mass: Cambridge University Press.

Law, John. 2004. *After Method: Mess in Social Science Research.* London: Routledge.

Linenthal, Edward 1991. *Sacred Ground: Americans and Their Battlefields.* Champaign: University of Illinois Press.

Mead, George H. 1934. *Mind, Self, and Society: From the Standpoint of a Social Behaviorist.* Chicago: University of Chicago Press.

Meinig, Donald. 1979. *The Interpretation of Ordinary Landscapes.* New York: Oxford University Press.

Moreland, J. 2001. *Archaeology and Text.* London: Duckworth.

Oakeshott, Michael. 1933. *Experience and its Modes.* Cambridge: Cambridge University Press.

Olivier, Laurent. 2001. *The Archaeology of the Contemporary Past* in V. Buchli and G. Lucas (Editors). *Archaeologies of the Contemporary Past.* London: Routledge, pp. 175-88.

2013. *The Business of Archaeology is in the Present* in *Re-Claiming Archaeology Beyond the Tropes of Modernity.* Edited by Alfredo Gonzalez-Ruibal. London: Routledge, pp. 117-129.

Pavis, P. 1998. *Dictionary of the Theatre: Terms, Concepts, and Analysis.* Toronto: University of Toronto Press.

Pawleta, M. 2011. *The Past Industry: Selected Aspects of the Commercialization of the Past and Products of*

Archaeological Knowledge in Contemporary Poland. Sprawozdaria Archaeological Reports 63: 9-54.

Pearson, Mike and Michael Shanks. 2001. *Theatre/Archaeology.* London: Routledge.

Pratt, M.I. 2008. *Imperial Eyes: Travel, Writing, and Transculturation.* London: Routledge.

Rose, Nikolas. 1998. *Inventing Our Selves: Psychology, Power, and Personhood.* Cambridge: Cambridge University Press.

Sabol, John G. 2012. *The Production of Haunted Space: Its Meaning and Excavation.* Bedford, Pennsylvania: Ghost Excavation Books, Inc.

2013. *The Ghost Excavation: An Ethnography of a Haunted Site.* Bedford, Pennsylvania: Ghost Excavation Books, Inc.

2013. *Burnside Bridge: The Excavation of a Civil War Soundscape.* Brunswick, Maryland: Ghost Excavation Books, Inc.

2014. *The Culture of War and the American Civil War.* Bedford, Pennsylvania: Ghost Excavation Books, Inc.

Sawyer, R.K. 2003. *Ground, Creativity, Music, Theater, Collaboration.* Mahwah, New Jersey: Lawrence Erlbaum.

Schechner, Richard. 1990. *Magnitudes of Performance* in R. Schechner and W. Appel (Editors) *By Means of Performance.* Cambridge: Cambridge University Press.

Schneider, Rebecca. 2012. *Performing Remains: Art and War in Times of Theatrical Reenactment.* London: Routledge.

Shanks, Michael. 2012. *The Archaeological Imagination.* Walnut Creek, California: Left Coast Press.

Straight, Belinda. 2007. *Sensing Divinity, Death, and Resurrection: Theorizing Experience Through Miracles* in *The Sixth Sense Reader.* David Howes (Editor). Oxford: Berg, pp. 325-337.

Strathern, M. 1991. *Partial Connections.* Savage, Maryland: Rowman and Littlefield.

Tilley, C. 1989. *Excavation as Theatre. Antiquity* 63: 275-280.

1991. *Material Culture and Text: The Art of Ambiguity.* London: Routledge.

1994. *A Phenomenology of Landscape: Places, Paths, and Monuments.* Oxford: Berg.

Trombley, Jeremy. 2012. *The Ontological Turn.* Weblog Post. Retrieved from Http://struggleforever.com/the-ontological-turn. April 26, 2014.

Turnbull, Colin. 1979. *The Mountain People.* New York: Simon & Schuster.

Viveiros, de Castro, Eduardo. 1998. *Cosmological Deixis and Amerindian Perspectivism.* Translated by Elizabeth Ewart. Journal of the Royal Anthropological Institute 4(3): 469-488.

Wallace, S. 2011. *Contradictions of Archaeological Theory: Engaging Critical Realism and Archaeological Theory. Archaeologia Aeliana* (5th Series) 26: 1-15.

Weber, Max. 1947. *The Theory of Social and Economic Organization.* New York: Free Press.

Yentsch, Ann. 1988. *Legends, Houses, Families, and Myths: Relationships Between Material Culture and American Ideology* in *Documentary Archaeology in the New World.* Mary Beaudry (Editor). Cambridge: Cambridge University Press, pp. 5-19.

Biography

11. Author, John G. Sabol

John Sabol is an archaeologist, cultural anthropologist, actor, and author. As an archaeologist, he has unearthed past material remains in excavations and site surveys in England, Mexico, and at various sites in the United States (including Eastern South Dakota, the Tennessee River Valleys, and in Pennsylvania). His anthropological fieldwork includes the studies of "spirits" in the religious beliefs of the afterlife among various cultural groups in Mexico (Mixtec, Zapotec, Lacandon, Nahuatl, and Otomi). His acting career includes "ghosting" performances of various characters and scenarios in more than 35 movies, TV shows, and documentaries. He has appeared in the A&E TV series, Paranormal State as an investigative consultant.

He has written twenty-one books. These include: ***Ghost Excavator (2007), Ghost Culture (2007), Gettysburg Unearthed (2007), Battlefield Hauntscape (2008), The Anthracite Coal Region: The Archaeology of its Haunting Presence (2008), The Politics of Presence: Haunting Performances on the Gettysburg Battlefield (2008), Bodies of Substance, Fragments of Memories: An Archaeological Sensitivity to Ghostly Presence (2009), Phantom Gettysburg (2009), Digging Deep: An Archaeologist Unearths a Haunted Life (2009), The Re-Hauntings of Gettysburg (2010), Digging Up Ghosts (2011), The Haunted Theatre (2011), Haunting Archaeologies (2012), Beyond the Paranormal: Unearthing An Extended "Normal" at Haunted Locations (2013), Burnside Bridge Hauntscape: The Excavation of a Civil War Soundscape (2013), The Gettysburg Battlefield Experience (2013), The Good Death and The Civil War (2014), Centralia: A Vision of Ruin (2014).***

His recent speaking engagements include the T.A.G. (Theoretical Archaeology Group) Conference at the University of California, Berkeley, at the Space and Place Conference in Prague, Czech Republic, the TAG

Conference at the University in Buffalo, New York, Exploring the Extraordinary Conference in York, England, the C.H.A.T. archaeological conference also in York, and the GHost Conference at the University of London, London, England.

His investigative reports have been published in such diverse venues as Haunted Times Magazine, Tennessee Anthropologist, and the online journal, ParaAnthropology. He has been a frequent guest on numerous radio and internet talk shows, among them, Beyond the Edge Radio, The Paranormal View, Para X Radio, Blog Talk Radio, The Grand Dark Conspiracy, and Rusty O'Nhiall's "Mysterious and Unexplained" on PsiFM (Australia). He was a university professor in Mexico for 11 years, teaching both undergraduate and graduate courses on the anthropology of tourism. He has also been featured on public educational TV for U.S. and foreign markets, and has worked on international educational documentaries (in Spain).

He has a M.A. in Anthropology/Archaeology (University of Tennessee), and a B.A. in Sociology/Anthropology (Bloomsburg University). He has also attended Penn State University, the University of Pittsburgh, the University of the Americas (Cholula, Puebla, Mexico), and has studied theatre and method acting in Mexico City.

He can be reached via email at cuicospirit@hotmail.com. His website is: **www.ghostexcavation.com** and he can be found on Facebook ("Ghost Excavations with John Sabol").

www.ingramcontent.com/pod-product-compliance
Lightning Source LLC
Chambersburg PA
CBHW071358310526
45789CB00020B/528